Occultism

The Ultimate Guide to the Occult, Including Magic, Divination, Astrology, Witchcraft, and Alchemy

Your Free Gift (only available for a limited time)

Thanks for getting this book! If you want to learn more about various spirituality topics, then join Mari Silva's community and get a free guided meditation MP3 for awakening your third eye. This guided meditation mp3 is designed to open and strengthen ones third eye so you can experience a higher state of consciousness. Simply visit the link below the image to get started.

https://spiritualityspot.com/meditation

Contents

INTRODUCTION 1

CHAPTER ONE: WHAT IS THE OCCULT? 3

    EVOLUTION OF THE OCCULT 4

    NEW AGE OCCULTISM 8

    BRANCHES OF OCCULTISM 10

    MISCONCEPTIONS ABOUT OCCULTISM 11

CHAPTER TWO: MODERN WITCHCRAFT 13

    DISTINCTION BETWEEN WICCANS AND PAGANS 14

    COVENS, COVENSTEADS, AND COVENDOMS 15

    HIVES: NOT JUST A TERM FOR BEES 16

    WHAT A COVEN IS NOT 17

    THE ROLE OF THE LEADERS IN COVENS 18

    TYPES OF WITCHES 20

CHAPTER THREE: ACTIVATING YOUR INNER WITCH 24

    SIGNS YOU MIGHT BE A WITCH 24

    BASIC WITCHCRAFT TERMINOLOGY 27

    POPULAR MISCONCEPTIONS ABOUT WITCHES 34

    THE LUNAR PHASES AND THEIR SIGNIFICANCE TO WITCHCRAFT 37

    INTERMEDIATE OR SECONDARY PHASES OF THE MOON 38

    BEST DAYS FOR MOON MAGIC 39

CHAPTER FOUR: TOOLS OF THE CRAFT 41

Beginner Magic Tools 41

Cleaning and Storing Magical Tools 47

Charging Tools and Crystals 47

Popular Magical Herbs and Their Uses.. 48

Popular Magical Trees 50

Useful Apps for the Budding Witch 51

CHAPTER FIVE: BUILDING YOUR ALTAR 53

Sacred Circles Versus Altars.. 54

Altar Location.. 55

Cleansing the Space for Your Altar.. 55

To Decorate or Not to Decorate?.. 57

Flower Power for Your Altar 59

Tending to Your Altar 60

Rituals for the Budding Witch 61

CHAPTER SIX: KEEPING A GRIMOIRE OR BOOK OF SHADOWS 63

The Origin of The Book of Shadows 63

The Grimoire and Its History 64

Famous Ancient Grimoires 65

Types of Grimoires 68

Questions to Ask Yourself Before Starting a Grimoire/Book of
Shadows... 69

Inclusion Criteria 70

Keeping a Grimoire 71

Organizing Your Book of Shadows (BOS).................................. 72

Organization Tips for Your Book 72

The Digital BOS 73

Crafting Your Grimoire 74

The Difference Between a BOS and a Grimoire 75

BOS/Grimoire Security 76

CHAPTER SEVEN: UNLOCKING DIVINATION AND PSYCHIC POWERS...79

Choosing a System... 80

Popular Forms of Divination 81

Divination Spells.. 87

CHAPTER EIGHT: THE POWER OF INVOCATION 89

WHAT INVOCATION IS 89

PURPOSES OF INVOCATION 91

THE CONCEPT OF EVOCATION 93

THE DIFFERENCE BETWEEN INVOCATION AND EVOCATION.........................94

TO INVOKE, EVOKE, OR DO BOTH? 95

CHAPTER NINE: CRYSTAL MAGIC AND ALCHEMY 98

FORMS OF CRYSTAL ENERGY..98

VERSATILE STONES EVERYONE SHOULD OWN 99

SOME SPELLS FOR CRYSTAL MAGIC 106

CHAPTER TEN: CREATING YOUR SPELLS AND RITUALS...................108

CRAFTING YOUR SPELLS..108

STEPS TO CREATING A FOOLPROOF SPELL..109

THE RELEVANCE OF CORRESPONDENCE IN SPELL CRAFTING 112

THE ETHICS OF SPELLCASTING 113

ETHICAL OUTS..114

CONCLUSION..117

HERE'S ANOTHER BOOK BY MARI SILVA THAT YOU MIGHT
LIKE..119

YOUR FREE GIFT (ONLY AVAILABLE FOR A LIMITED TIME) 120

REFERENCES 121

Introduction

"The occult" is a phrase that terrifies most people needlessly. Depending on how you look at it, people are under the impression that occultists just draw pentagrams, possess an array of tools with varying levels of sharpness, and dine with his majesty the devil every Friday night on a full moon. Sure, that whole sentence may read like an overstatement, but a lot of people shy away from the occult because they find it flat out scary, no thanks to all the misinformation out there.

You clearly aren't like a lot of people. You're reading this because you know on an intuitive level that there's more to occultism, magic, astrology, divination, witchcraft, and alchemy than meets the eye. Science may work tirelessly to prove that these things are nothing more than hobbies at best and mindless fantasies at worst. They might try to insist that there is nothing beyond the physical world of matter and that there is no other way to manipulate things in the universe than through good old-fashioned action, but you've known for a while now that that's most definitely not the case.

This book is designed to answer some pressing questions concerning the occult. Written with the novice and intermediate reader in mind, it covers areas of occultism, mysticism, crystal magic, and so much more in an explanatory and unbiased manner.

The purpose of this book is to change the narrative concerning the occult and witchcraft as a whole. The lady who works at your favorite bagel store, the bartender at your local pub, your next-door neighbor, or the cute man at the carwash might be a witch or some other form of Pagan or occultist. And no, that doesn't make them bad people. In fact, occultists are some of the most wonderful folk you'll ever meet. Pagans are not the devil's minions. Besides, one should not mock the desire to serve in the old ways.

No author (including myself) can write a book and claim it's a comprehensive representation of Wiccan culture and the occult mindset. The craft is continually evolving. Each occultist decides within himself or herself what and how best to practice their devotion to the divine. I will discuss the core beliefs, ethical principles, practices, and opinions accepted by most while dispelling popular misconceptions about occultism.

Now here's a fair bit of warning: knowledge is pointless and powerless if you don't put it into action. So, what you want to do is read this book once for clarity, and then come back to it again, paying particular attention to the portions that drew you in the most as you read. Then put what you learn into practice. Above all else, you should learn to be a lifelong student. See what else you can learn and put it to the ultimate test by practicing and seeing what results you get. After all, books are pointless if you don't gain your own personal experience with the occult and the spiritual. With your own experience, you never have to question or wonder about the validity of these things, and no one can shake your beliefs. This means you will only get better and better at practicing your craft, which is the ultimate path to spiritual growth.

Chapter One: What is the Occult?

The word "occult" originates from the late 15th-century Latin word "occultus" and the middle French "occulte," being the past participle of "occulere." All of this translates to mean "clandestine, secret, covered over, hidden, or to shut off from view."

Occultism was linked to paranormal studies, including astrology, alchemy, magic, precognition, telekinesis, necromancy, and metaphysics, in the late 16th century. The earliest known use of the word "occultism" in English texts is in an article titled "A Few Questions to Hiraf" published in 1875 by the *Spiritual Scientist*, an American spiritualist magazine. A Russian immigrant and founder of theosophy named Helena Blavatsky wrote this article while living in the United States. In its broadest sense, occultism is a variety of paranormal practices and beliefs bordering magic, mysticism, and spirituality. It's also linked to otherworldly concepts such as parapsychology, extrasensory perception, psychometry, and psychokinesis.

Occultism is the opposite of apocalypse, from the Greek word "apokalyptein," a spiritual term denoting revelation or disclosure. This reason is why religious denominations regard occultism as the antithesis of the divine. An occultist is a devotee to the science of gaining spiritual knowledge far beyond the physical realm and the tentacles of science.

Countless opinions and postulations exist regarding the understanding and practice of mystic beings and extramundane forces. Such beings, powers, and customs—primarily divinatory and otherworldly—have been in existence and are documented in history, although with substantial discrepancies in their make-up and public perspective.

This science has recently come under fire and vilification because it suggests practices and nuances that disagree with the widespread version of normal." To the layman, the focal point of occultism is the expert's supposed ability to influence or orchestrate the laws of nature and morality for their own, or another's benefit.

Anthropologists opine it is impossible to distinguish between religion and magic, the principal constituent of occult belief. This is the case of various religious sects of individual societies. Though, this opinion holds no water as many religious groups view natural laws and morality as clear-cut in their own right.

Evolution of the Occult

The 19th and 20th century narrative of the supernatural in the West impacted the current view of occultism. The 16th and 17th centuries had people believing in the existence of supernatural forces and entities. The prevalence of forces beyond human control brought solace to some, and terror, suffering, and death to others. Many occult practitioners reigned supreme by virtue of their right to control these psychic powers.

Events that unfolded led to the holy inquisition and texts like Malleus Maleficarum, which served to terminate the lives of hundreds if not thousands of Satanists, witches, and other "heretics." The torture and persecution of occultists led to an increase in certain dishonest religious clerics' efforts to mislead the public with bogus miracles and objects of virtue. The 16th and 17th centuries brought about a severe review of controversial supernatural occurrences starting with artifacts and, much later, the witch hunters' exploits.

Western occultism is an old secret belief underlying all occult practices. This hidden philosophy originates from alchemy and Hellenistic magic on the one hand, and Jewish spiritualism on the other. The primary source of Hellenistic magic is the text written by Hermes Trismegistus, the *Corpus Hermeticum*, and this treatise contains gnosis, astrology, alchemy, magic, and other mystic sciences favoring spiritual regeneration. Its doctrines were instrumental in the evolution of Wicca, modern neo-Paganism, and Western magic.

Jewish mysticism is supported by the Kabbalah, which is made up of teachings on esoteric mysticism. The Zohar, written in medieval Hebrew and Aramaic, is a compendium of mystical commentaries on the Torah and is the Kabbalah's backbone. Jewish metaphysical thought was known to European scholars in the Middle Ages and was associated with the Corpus Hermeticum through the Renaissance. The ensuing Hermetic-Kabbalistic custom was called Hermeticism, which was integrated into an ideology and magical practice (the latter occurring as natural and positive magic in contradiction to the "negative magic" supplied by witchcraft or sorcery).

The science of alchemy incorporated Hermeticism, which was reinforced with the emergence of Rosicrucianism in the early 17th century. The Rosicrucians were a covert society that used alchemical symbols and passed on arcane wisdom to followers, building a spiritual alchemy method that continued past the advancement of theoretical science and allowed Hermetism to progress smoothly into the Age of Enlightenment (1715 - 1789).

In the 18th century, Freemasons adopted occultism, as they didn't find a suitable occult doctrine in Freemasonry. These esoterically inclined enthusiasts persevered as lone students of Hermeticism and as occult groups in Continental Europe into the 19th century, when religious cynicism caused a rise in the rebuffing of Orthodox doctrines by the enlightened. This, in turn, led to an accompanying search for redemption by any other means, including occultism.

As Protestantism lost social and cultural significance while scientific observation and the study of natural phenomena gained ground, general mistrust was created. Later in the 18th century, this mistrust gave birth to Deism, a school of thought that confirmed the belief that God was the creator of natural law.

Deism was restricted to only a select few powerful and influential members of society such as George Washington, Benjamin Franklin, and other founding fathers of America. The 19th century made the doubtful view of mysticism the bedrock of "free thought." Freethinkers influenced all forms of theological and academic thinking at the time. This period's events had preachers in heated arguments with confirmed atheists, theologians proving God's existence, and missionaries doubling their attempts to influence the faithless.

Even with the reemergence of mysticism in the 19th century, occultism failed to gain ground in academic factions even though it impacted famous artists like Wassily Kandinsky, Austin Osman Spare, and the poet William Butler Yeats from time to time.

In light of all this, it is safe to say the definition of occultism has gone from being shrouded in mystery and hidden knowledge to the uninitiated, to bearing different meanings and several misconceptions. In the heated debate between the religious and the free thinkers, a small sect who prefers to be called "Spiritualists" put forward a new perspective. They state that the difference between this life and the life beyond is a theory of our own making, as everything known, and unknown is part of this universe. Spiritualists sought the help of seers to access the supernatural realm and relay messages that could not have been gotten via scientific means.

The seers channeled a variety of psychic phenomena, pointing to the presence of unseen forces functioning in the physical plane; powers unknown and undocumented by the scientific bodies prevalent at the time. Thus, with the advent and advancement of spiritualism, some academics with close ties to religion and scientific methods presumed scientific observation could be used in studying paranormal sightings, especially concerning hauntings, apparitions, and ghosts. This idea birthed England's Ghost Club in 1862, and several investigations were conducted on supernatural sightings over the next two decades. In 1882, New Age researchers started the London Society for Psychical Research to observe the goings-on in spiritual seances and other paranormal phenomena.

The timeline from 1882 to 1939—the start of the Second World War—marked a turbulent alliance between psychic research and Spiritualism. Spiritualism and its branches (primarily Theosophy) exposed the psychic phenomena researchers cataloged and experimented with. They understood that these happenings, if proven, had extensive consequences for understanding the world and its machinations.

Piles of data were gathered, both positive and negative. Evidence documenting a plethora of supernatural occurrences that buttress mortal-spirit contact was compiled. Simultaneously, it was discovered that most of the information gathered by mediums like telekinesis and mind over matter materializations were often counterfeit. This rising incidence of trickery, even by seers seen as genuine, created a quandary.

These occurrences caused many to question the standing of Spiritualism. Though it didn't outright declare every medium or occult practitioner a fraud, it implied that the occult movement sheltered crooks and encouraged their profession, even with glaring evidence of foul play. It also classified psychic researchers who generated any positive proof as gullible, lackadaisical, and–even worse–aides to con artists masquerading as mediums.

This was the highlight of the literary works of Lewis Spence and Nandor Fodor. The former published his book titled the *Encyclopedia of Occultism and Parapsychology*, which spoke of psychic phenomena from a Spiritualist perspective, stating his hope for scientists to discover the technique for authenticating supernatural incidents.

Fodor's *Encyclopedia of Psychic Sciences* was published a decade after this. This book admitted to the presence of artifice and deception in Spiritualism, but he believed in the information gathered by notable psychic researchers and other colleagues.

Half a century after Fodor and Spence's publications, the occult and metaphysical have adopted a new face. A face supported by the "New Age" movement.

The ideas surrounding Theosophy, Spiritualism, and supernatural phenomena have been entirely affected by the discovery of parapsychology. The induction of the Parapsychological Association into the American Academy for Scientific Advancement allowed for honesty and transparency with mystical research by the scientific community, since parapsychologists became more orthodox, renouncing most of the data gathered from earlier research.

New Age Occultism

In ancient times, occult phenomena and deviations from natural law were connected with mysterious entities, souls of the departed, and other unseen entities. Rituals were conducted to stave off misfortune, gain knowledge of past or future events, accumulate wealth, cause harm to one's foes, and awaken spirits and entities. Indigenous cultures have always associated occult practices with shamans, conjurers, and other practitioners with supernatural abilities.

In the late 20th century, sometime around 1970, there was a surge in occult practice. 1980 saw the dawn of the New Age Coalition. The growing curiosity in metaphysical thought and supernatural events led to the rise of channeling, using crystals, belief in angels, and exorcism rituals. Regardless of fads, the field of parapsychology has become entrenched in mainstream society in ways no one could have imagined in the 50s.

After the fall of the Roman Empire in the Middle Ages, the early Church tried to control the people. Its strategy was to berate any practice that wasn't in line with the Church's precepts. While more people converted to Christianity, the old ways remained and were practiced in utmost secrecy. At this point, any practice outside the Christian faith's strict confines was deemed dark and occult. The Church decided that any ceremony, science, or art form that defied rational interpretation was categorized as occult.

The mystic arts may have terrified some people, but the Middle Ages saw the separation of occultism from religion and its competition with mainstream religious practices. Many rituals and magical spells of the Middle Ages are based on pre-Christian beliefs in Mediterranean countries.

One's outlook on the plausibility of supernatural occurrences and the occult is dependent on one's religious or philosophical standpoint. For instance, Allan Kardec's theory of Spiritism is a branch of Spiritualism that believes in reincarnation. Spiritism and Spiritualism are essentially religious schools of thought, both certifying biblical miracles and specifying paranormal events as true and valid.

The metaphysical is still regarded as "occult" even today. Since the Middle Ages, occultism has become the derogatory label used in describing numerous supernatural associations or groups, all of which have several underlying traits such as: a set of rituals or practices; the education of members on the history; secret knowledge; and philosophical principles guiding them.

The New Age movement has refuted these claims by reforming the occult. Divination activities such as tarot card reading, astrology, numerology, palmistry, tasseography, scrying, and rune casting have been designated as counseling practices, while Wiccans have banded together to refute anti-witchcraft activities, discrediting them as religious fanaticism.

Interested groups aligned themselves with newer blends of occult science, like Hyperanism. Some embrace Theosophy, a mix of Western and Eastern occultism, while others turn to Spiritualism, which allows contact between the living and the dead via a medium.

Branches of Occultism

The values of the Church still define neo-occultism. *The Complete Evangelism Guidebook* categorizes the broad practice of occultism into three groups, namely:

- **Divinatory Practices:** This branch of occult science pursues hidden knowledge, usually about the past or near future, using psychic readings and other mystical methods. Divinatory aids include palmistry, scrying with crystals or tea leaves, astrology, and other divination tools.

- **Paganism:** This is often called Neo-Paganism and is distinctly different from the flourishing revival of ancient Paganism, which began in the 19th century. The 1960s saw the inception of Animism, the attribution of a living soul to places, creatures, or inanimate objects. Animism pays reverence to ancient deities like Gaia or Mother Earth.

- **Spiritism:** Spiritism and Spiritualism are often used interchangeably, but there are marked differences in these practices. Firstly, Spiritualism began with the Fox sisters, Leah, Margaretta, and Catherine, in 1848. The French academic Hippolyte Leon Denizard Rivail (also known as Allan Kardec) started Spiritism in 1850. Spiritism is, therefore, a subsidiary of Spiritualism. Spiritualists and Spiritists believe discarnate entities and humans can communicate and carry on relationships. Only Spiritists believe in reincarnation and the evolution of souls. In contrast, Spiritualists claim reincarnation is impossible as it cuts off the link between the living and our departed beloved. Spiritualism believes in the existence of God, but Spiritism has no formal religious background. Both are similar because they both have roots in the occult and require a belief in the paranormal. Spiritualism persisted in modern times, following the popularity of seances from the mid-1800s to 1920.

Misconceptions About Occultism

Over the years, occultism has been painted with a brushstroke of evil and forbidden activities. The following are the most common misconceptions that exist regarding occult science.

- **Science is Part of the Occult:** Science was highly misunderstood during the Middle Ages, and for this reason, it was branded an occult practice by religious sects. The interactions between elements and chemicals or between substances and objects were poorly understood and branded "magic." Herbalists were "practitioners of Earth magic," as they dealt with controlling and altering natural elements. Alchemists were branded "witches" or "warlocks" because they possessed the ability to modify metals and other elements using heat and other extraordinary processes.

- **Cults and the Occult are the Same:** Many people consider Christianity to be a religious cult itself. Some groups who were once seen as cults have historically and socially evolved to become religious groups. Examples are the Seventh Day Adventists, led at one time by Ellen White, and the Mormons, led by Joseph Smith.

Some argue that the word "cult" is nothing but a defamatory label used against new religious movements and their adherents. Cults are sects with firmly entrenched beliefs and power revolving around a single leader. This fanatical following requires a group of people, a high level of exclusivity, and commitments that are not typical of other groups.

On the other hand, the occult is a system of secret beliefs and principles that do not require a group of people. A single person can be an occultist. Occultism is the search for the truth, while cults have no desire for enlightenment. Using "cult" and "occult" interchangeably is a damaging misconception and a fallacy of generalization.

• **Occultism is Synonymous with Satanism:** A general misconception is that all Satanists are occultists and vice versa. This goes back to the Church's definition of the occult and other ancient secret practices. Theistic Satanism is a belief that regards Satan or Lucifer as an impartial supernatural force or deity deserving of veneration and adoration. Satanists view their religion as a spiritual path of knowledge, the individuality of thought, and self-development. The Church's stance on occultism is regarded as insincere and sanctimonious, mostly when seen through the Christian Classics Ethereal Library lens. The Church has professed an uninterrupted string of miraculous abilities, like demon exorcism, the gift of tongues, power of prophecy, and raising the dead. Following this definition, the Church itself should be considered occult and likened to Satanism.

Chapter Two: Modern Witchcraft

American theosophist David Spangler founded the New Age movement in 1970. This movement is an array of religious or spiritual practices and beliefs that spread quickly in the West in the 1970s. Spangler believed specific astrological changes brought about a release of new waves of powerful spiritual energy, propelling the Earth into what he called the "age of Aquarius."

The New Age is a form of Western esotericism that draws from ancient cultures, particularly the occultist movements of the 18th and 19th centuries, mostly practiced then among middle and upper-middle-class backgrounds. Theosophy, Freemasonry, Spiritualism, the UFO religions of the 1950s, the Human Potential Movement, the counterculture of the 1960s, and works of mystics like Franz Anton Mesmer and Emanuel Swedenborg all heavily influenced the early period.

New Ageism reigned supreme in the United Kingdom in the 1970s and spread to America between the 1980s and 1990s. The premier advocate of this movement in America was Ram Dass. Claims by channelers like J.Z Knight (who channels Ramtha), Jane Roberts (who channeled Seth), and Jach Pursel (who channels Lazarus) have promoted the growth of the New Age phenomenon. The *Seth*

Material sold over a million copies in the US alone, making New Age ideas more accessible to the public.

Traditional tools of the occult such as astrology, tarot reading, yoga, meditation, and mediumship were introduced into the New Age movement to help in personal development and transformation, but two tools used heavily at this time were crystals and mediums.

Many "New Agers" acknowledge Source (the divine being who is the originator of all things) and a Higher Self infused with the Divine essence of creation. There is also an assortment of entities like ascended masters, devas, extraterrestrials, spirit guides, and angels who commune with mortals through channeling. In addition, there's a clear emphasis on healing through unorthodox medicine and a belief in merging science and spirituality.

In the mid-1990s, the New Age movement found its way to Canada, New Zealand, Western Europe, America, and Australia. In 2015, the religious scholar Hugh Urban stated that New Age spiritualism was steadily increasing in the States as more and more people in America tick the "spiritual, not religious" box. New Age spiritualism promises freedom, autonomy over belief, spirit, soul, and body.

Distinction Between Wiccans and Pagans

Wicca is a religion of bliss and love, quite unlike Christianity, with its concept of "original sin" and the possibility of joy only in the afterlife. It's a nature-based neo-Pagan path popularized by Gerald Brosseau Gardner, with practices derived from pre-Christian traditions. Wiccans worship the Mother Goddess and her consort, the Horned God. Today, Wicca is one of the fastest spreading religions in the States.

The word "Pagan" originates from the Latin word "Paganus," meaning "a countryside dweller" and the Latin "pagus," meaning "rural district." In the same way, the word "heathen" initially referred to a person living on the heath. Paganism represents the way many people practiced religion and spirituality before the advent of Christianity. It describes beliefs that don't conform to any main-world religion such as Hinduism, Christianity, or Islam. "Pagan" was the word used by Christians in the early fourth century to describe people who worshipped more than one God.

Paganism and Heathenism had negative connotations, but that has changed in recent times. Pagan customs were a way of nudging nature in a positive direction to aid the survival of the tribe. Later on, these rituals graduated into full-time symbolic festivities marked in calendars. Puritans imbued their beliefs into already celebrated Pagan traditions to enable an easy transition to Christianity. This is why the Winter Solstice and the Roman Saturnalia became "Christmas," the Spring Equinox became "Easter," and the Roman Lupercalia festival became "Saint Valentine's Day," et cetera.

Covens, Covensteads, and Covendoms

In Wicca and many forms of neo-Pagan witchcraft, a coven is a community of witches or Wiccans who gather together for meetings, rituals, or to perform magical ceremonies. It is a Priesthood comprised of both genders, usually in the same district or village, and presided over by a leader. The word "coven" originates from the Anglo-Norman word "covent," and the Latin "conventum."

Coven members are bound by law to attend weekly meetups called "esbat." A covenstead is where members of a coven meet and store religious paraphernalia. Covendoms are territories where witches live, extending to a 3 to 6-mile radius in all directions from a covenstead so that the covensteads do not overlap each other. The distance halfway between one covenstead and the next is the covendom radius.

The uninitiated are called a "cowan." Cowans are unable to attend Wiccan gatherings, although some sects give allowance for visitors to observe rites. They believe it is a great idea to allow cowans to sit in at religious ceremonies (not magical ones) to experience the true spirit of the Old Religion; get rid of any misconceptions they have about the faith; and maybe be enticed to join the path.

After initiation, you become a witch and a Priestess or Priest, meaning you can conduct your magical rites and strike out alone. In Gardnerian Wicca, the High Priestess is referred to as Lady Her-Name-Here. Whichever coven you choose to belong to, you must take their duties and rites to heart. If any doubts arise about what these rights and responsibilities are, then the High Priestess or Priest should be consulted personally.

Neo-Pagan groups that are neither Druid nor Wiccan prefer the term "circle" or "temple" instead of "coven" because it is safe and non-specific. None of these terms are copyrighted, so it is possible under the law to call your group whatever you wish. Still, to avoid confusion, refrain from using the term "coven" unless your gathering comprises Wiccans or witches.

Hives: Not Just a Term for Bees

The number of members in a coven may differ. Two witches are a "working couple" regardless of gender, and a gathering of at least three can form a coven. Some covens contain seven members of both genders, but according to Murray's theories, the ideal number is thirteen. Wiccans believe that a coven larger than thirteen is cumbersome and could create turbulence in group dynamics. For this reason, when a coven grows to an unmanageable extent, it may hive or split to form a new coven with leaders who have completed a third-degree initiation.

Hiving off could be a joyous occasion where the mother and daughter coven still meet for rituals and work side by side during festivities. Or it could be a spiteful action on the part of some members dissatisfied with the workings of the mother coven. If you plan on starting your coven, the safest way is to join an existing coven to get some experience before branching out on your own.

What a Coven is Not

- **A Coven Isn't a Clique:** A clique comprises members who drop by whenever they are idle or have nothing better to focus their energies on. Cliques are appreciated when you want to find friends or network without regard for the group's focus. This mentality does not apply to covens. Covens are made up of members who work well together and are willing to put in the time, dedication, and hard work to progress through magical arts.

- **It Isn't a Proxy for a Family:** Families contain people who tolerate each other and who sometimes may or may not love each other. Family members are part of a unit that is usually not of their own making. This is why the conflict that exists within a family can consume a substantial portion of time and effort. On the other hand, a coven is a unit of people with similar interests who respect each other and work seamlessly together. It's not perfect, but each person in the coven has individual family units and personal troubles. "Coveners" are bonded over spiritual matters, and biological family issues are set aside for the benefit of the whole. In the same vein, do not let coven matters make you neglect your family.

- **It Isn't a Church:** Covens might be gatherings for worship, but they aren't Churches. Churches are Christian, while witchcraft or Wicca isn't. Covens do not have paid Clergy. Instead, they have High Priests and Priestesses to encourage spiritual growth. Everyone in Wicca is considered a

Priest or Priestess. This differentiates it from Orthodox religion that proposes a single individual to be an indispensable part of communion with Gods or spirits. Coven leaders only serve to guide and teach each member to draw on the powers of God and nature for their benefit.

- **Covens Aren't Your Typical School:** In covens, you can learn the Old Religion, the art of healing, and magic. There are by-laws and a creed known as the Wiccan Rede. That being said, it is far from a conventional school. There are no formal classrooms, curriculums, textbooks, or syllabi. No grades or exams are given to mark progress. Enlightenment is via oral means, constantly ongoing without any pressure whatsoever to learn. As such, students must be self-motivated. In a coven, you attain knowledge through experiences and meditation. No two people have the same experience, so there is no comparison between students. Your journey as a witch or Wiccan is personal and unique.

- **It Isn't Therapy:** Covens are not 12-step programs that help you tackle problems you cannot solve alone. It is wrong to assume that entry into a coven automatically solves all your issues. To achieve success as a witch or Wiccan, you must be willing to take steps to build a relationship with the Gods yourself. Many witches seek professional help from therapists in dealing with personal challenges, and there's no reason to be ashamed of that.

The Role of the Leaders in Covens

A coven, like every other group, requires a leader who is the High Priest or High Priestess. Leaders could even be a couple made up of either or different sexes. A Priest represents the Horned God, while the Priestess the Goddess, whether it's the Moon Goddess or the Earth Goddess. In Saxon tradition, leaders are selected following a unanimous vote of all members and serve for a year before reelection. Some covens advocate rotating leadership or democracy within the ranks to prevent members from abusing power.

No leader possesses more power than the members. They are all equal in their own right. This system of selecting leaders has several advantages. It prevents power plays, favoritism, and ego trips by members of the coven in power. This allows everyone a chance to lead the coven at some point and makes it easy to remove leaders who abuse their position, as well as reinstate leaders who serve the coven well.

Some covens use a degree-based selection for leaders. New coveners are initiated into first-degree duties: like lighting up the candles for sacred circles, filling up the goblets, and chanting hymns for rituals. As you rise through the ranks to the third degree, you stand the chance of being considered a High Priest or Priestess.

A sacred circle is a holy space where energies are concentrated and retained to perform holy rites or keep the undesirable entities out. The purpose of the circle determines its dimensions and how many members will be in it.

Witches can become High Priestesses or Priests by hiving off to form their own covens or by appointment to replace a leader who has passed or has been forced to step down. High Priestesses are responsible for the coven's day-to-day operations, and they make sure that all coveners work well with one another.

Many magical rituals require the use of psychic powers. This is why apart from good leadership qualities and charisma, High Priestesses must possess great intuition, empathy, and strong psychic powers, to help other members come into their abilities, bend and shape these powers, and sense when they are at their zenith.

It is also the work of the High Priestess to sanctify the magic circle, call upon deities, elementals, and cardinal spirits. They are responsible for leading dances, chants, and spell work in the coven. They also delegate specific duties to coveners capable of fulfilling them as part of their training.

The Maiden, a second-degree witch with some level of experience, stands in for the High Priestess in dire situations. Still, her main task is administrative, like a Human Relations Manager helping to train new initiates and serving as a personal assistant to the High Priestess, among other duties. The Maiden office is held by a single woman until she either succeeds the High Priestess or hives off to form a separate coven. Some covens also have a Summoner who serves as the information manager, charged with scheduling esbat and notifying coveners.

Types of Witches

When starting out, it is not essential to label yourself outright. Getting to know the kind of witch you are will take some time. You need to discover your interests and what resonates with you. Even with this discovery, witchcraft is continuously evolving. Labels are not necessary, but they serve a purpose. They represent a way of claiming identity and ownership of your craft. Labels exist for that only, so it is unnecessary to get wound up about what faction you belong to. That being said, here are some labels that some witches go by:

- **The Hereditary Witch:** A witch born into a family of witches. They may practice the craft even if they follow a different Wiccan path to that of their ancestors. Hereditary Wiccans are brought up with the skill, like the fictional character Sabrina Spellman, or they decide to embrace witchcraft later on in life. They may choose to practice alone or as part of a coven.

- **The Green Witch:** This witch is heavily attuned to Earth and nature magic. The green witch is a healer, a naturalist, and a nurturer. This category of witch understands the magical and medicinal properties of plants and herbs and includes garden witches, kitchen witches, hearth witches, and herbal witches. They specialize in practical magic for everyday ailments, cooking and brewing potions, antidotes, salves, and even poisons, by utilizing the power in plants and food to manipulate energy and create change.

- **The Hedge Witch:** One who practices her craft between this world and the world beyond. Extremely rare and very solitary, these witches are usually creative or artistically inclined, skilled at working with animals, familiars, time travel, psychometry, and spirit communication. They are also called astral witches, as their craft has elements of shamanism, herbalism, and astral projection.

- **The Glam Witch:** This is a witch who specializes in spinning a wheel of confidence and sizzling sensuality. They can attract attention to or away from themselves. This is ideal for camouflage and seduction. They are devotees of the Goddess Lilith and use crystals, the moon, scents, colors, glamour, and sex magic.

- **The Gem Witch:** Gem witchcraft is also called crystal witchcraft and is a branch of green witchcraft. These witches are in love with the Earth and geology. They possess an in-depth knowledge of crystals and gemstones and can harness their power for healing, ritualistic purposes, communion with the spirit world, and protection.

- **The Cosmic Witch:** They practice astrology and other forms of celestial magic. Their kind of divination is strongly aligned with the stars and planets. Also, they can choose to work with herbs, oils, runes, or crystals.

- **The Traditional Witches:** Traditional witchcraft, also known as the Old Religion, covers a series of non-Wiccan forms of witchcraft influenced by folklore. It does not imply a belief as old as time, but a collection of practices inspired by communion with ancestors, participation in sacred mystical work, and fealty to a strict path. Guidelines are handed down through generations and are ideal for witches attuned to ceremonial magic and structure.

- **The Oracle or Diviner Witch:** They are skilled in all forms of divination from aeromancy, numerology, stichomancy, and tarot, to runes, crystal gazing, scrying, amathomancy, dream interpretation, and other forms of divination. They're usually clairvoyant and clairaudient.

- **The Eclectic Witch:** This witch practices a little of everything. In this category, witches follow more than one path, using beliefs that work for them and discarding those that don't.

- **The Swamp Witch:** Found in the rivers and bayous of the world and well versed in spirit communication and magical folklore, their craft is a hodgepodge of traditional Southern magic and voodoo. They are very skilled potion makers and extremely warm individuals, but never take their kindness for granted. Their ability to curse is legendary.

- **The Necromancer:** This witch practices communing with the dead either in the form of spirits or apparitions, bringing the dead to life for divination or ritualistic purposes. Necromancy is also referred to as "death magic," and it evolved from shamanism. The necromancers' spell work involves assistance from spirits of the dead.

- **The Solitary Witch:** This witch chooses to practice their craft in the privacy of their homes or some other designated space, without the need to commune with other witches in a coven. Many solitary witches participate in group festivities like Samhain, Beltane, Ostara, or Imbolc.

- **The Desert Witch:** This witch is also known as the witch of the waste. They are prevalent in the desert and work with sand, bones, and limited supplies. They possess an enviable collection of skulls and fossils, and are famous for befriending or taming exotic, dangerous animals, like snakes, coyotes, scorpions, et cetera.

- **The Sea Witch:** This witch hones her practice near water bodies, preferably the ocean, but a pond or lake may suffice. They are in tune with bodies of water and the creatures that dwell in them. They may choose to worship a deity or familiarize themselves with sea nymphs, water fairies, et cetera. They are also adept at predicting the weather and have a hobby of collecting seawater, rare seashells, and other marine-based objects.

- **The Elemental Witch:** This witch draws power from all the elements, namely air, fire, water, and earth. They have gained control over nature by elemental manipulation. This is one of the trickiest types of magic to master, as these elements can be benevolent or destructive depending on the witch's intentions and skill set.

Chapter Three: Activating Your Inner Witch

Witchcraft is a science, an art, and a way of life all at once. No longer a craft to be burnt alive for, the number of witches in recent times has increased rapidly. The American Academy of Religions recognizes Wicca and witchcraft as legitimate practices. According to the Pentagon, 1,511 soldiers in the Air Force and 354 in the US marines practice the craft. The American Department of Defense allows Wiccan soldiers to state their beliefs on their dog tags.

Signs You Might Be a Witch

1. You have a sixth sense that is always spot-on and can manifest your wishes or a person's presence.

2. You have a healing or calming aura.

3. You are fueled by compassion and a desire to help or serve people. You may find yourself in volunteer groups or soup kitchens, agitating for change in the world, and continually putting others' needs before your own.

4. You are the weird kid, the oddball, or maybe the black sheep in your family. You may feel like an outsider looking at the world from a window in your castle; find it hard to make new friends; and often feel exhausted being around too many people's energies for too long.

5. You dream in high definition and these dreams are not just figments of your imagination like everyone else's. They hold a more profound meaning, like messages from celestial guides.

6. You often hear whispers or voices from unseen sources. If you have ruled out schizophrenia and other mental disorders, you might be clairaudient. It is your choice to hone this psychic ability or to suppress it.

7. You can't help your connection to nature. You are at peace with it and have become one with it. Most witches understand the cycle of life and how everything is connected.

8. You are very self-aware, show more empathy than the average person, and are the living embodiment of walking a mile in another's shoes.

9. You have more than tact, as you seem always to know the right thing to say to a loved one in need and stay far away from drama.

10. People who hardly know you always find themselves seeking your opinion or coming to you for advice. You are everyone's "ride or die."

11. You may have had a near-death experience that puts you in a situation where you are more aware of the mysteries of the Earth and beyond.

12. You enjoy your own company and are not afraid to demand it. You love people, but understand you need time alone for spiritual growth and connection with your Higher Self.

13. You find the answers to life's puzzles in nature and feel comfortable and empowered in natural areas like the woods, beach, or a park. Your body and moods are aligned with the phases of the moon or changing seasons.

14. You are like a wisdom sponge, soaking up all knowledge of the paranormal and ancient healing arts. You might also be amazed by the wonders of the universe.

15. You love animals (even wild ones), and they are in turn drawn to you. Strays often follow you home. You find you can communicate with them.

16. You find insight and messages in energies, antiques, or appearances in your life.

17. You feel energy and auras better than most.

18. You find your wishes often come true, even those said in anger.

19. People may refer to you as an "old soul."

20. You can't help your penchant for collecting things. You are a packrat, constantly collecting bones, antiques, feathers, crystals, books, shells, and other pieces of earth energy. Things no "normal" person finds interesting.

21. You are captivated by the concept of death and what happens after people die, often feeling like loved ones are around you, sending love and light in one way or another.

If any or all of these signs pertain to your nature, then congratulations, you just might be a witch.

Basic Witchcraft Terminology

Like any other field, witchcraft has its own vocabulary. This list is not exhaustive, but here are a few of the terms you need to familiarize yourself with if you want to walk the walk.

Altar: This is an elevated surface for religious offerings and ceremonies, such as worship of the God and Goddess, chanting, and casting spells. Altars are often covered in a cloth adorned with magical symbols and ceremonial items like candles, incense, ash, liquids, chalices, symbols of the four elements, and so on. In Wicca and Pagan religions, altars are never used for blood sacrifice.

Amulet: This is an inanimate object infused with magic to protect its wearer from evil, illness, and bad luck. The word "amulet" comes from the Old Latin "amoletum," meaning "line of defense."

Ankh: The Egyptian symbol for life, regeneration, and immortality. It is often carved into amulets and talismans to dispel evil and bring good fortune.

Arrow Position: A stance similar to Eastern mudras and asanas. Common in Pagan or Wiccan rituals, where members place their feet together and raise their arms directly above their head with their palms touching.

Athame: A witch's ritual knife for ceremonial purposes. It is usually made of iron or steel, double-edged with a black hilt. The athame is a phallic symbol. Dipping it into a chalice represents the merging of male and female energies. It represents the air element in magic rituals and is used in marking magical circles, never for cutting. If there is a need to cut, witches use a bolline.

Auto-da-fé: This is Portuguese for "act of faith." It was a public ceremony held by the Spanish and Portuguese governments during the inquisition before pronouncing judgment. Punishment at this time came in many forms, but the most popular was burning to death.

A Year and a Day: The standard length of time in most Pagan traditions. In Wicca, it is the customary amount of time an initiate studies to move on to the next degree of witchcraft.

Baba Yaga: Also called the "bony legged one," Baba Yaga is a legendary Slavic witch who is known to offer to heal. Contrary to the terrible way she is painted, there is more to Baba Yaga. She brings a balance of death, rebirth, dark forests, sickness, and dying, as well as renewal, healing, and profound wisdom. Her energy is strongest in autumn, from just before Mabon and Samhain.

Befana: This is the good witch in Italian folklore known to bring gifts to children on Epiphany. Other countries have Santa Claus.

Bell, Book, and Candle: This originated from a Catholic practice of excommunicating witches. The ringing of a bell signifies a death toll, and the closing of a book (the Bible) and the snuffing out of a candle represent the removal of a person's soul from God's sight.

Besom: This is the witch's broom. The bristles are arranged in a circle and made of twigs fastened to a stick.

Black Book: Now called the Book of Shadows, following Gardner's influence, witches initially used the "Black Book" to write down recipes, chants, and spells.

Blessed Be: A famous Wiccan salutation, often shortened to "BB."

Bodkin: Pin-like instruments used in torturing witches. Bodkins were used during the witch-burning frenzy when witches were accused of selling their souls to the Devil for power and possessing a mark (the Devil's mark) on their bodies. According to the oppressive Church and government, having the Devil's mark meant the witch would feel no pain and never bleed. Bodkins were used in poking witches until such spots on their bodies were discovered.

Bolline: A crescent-shaped knife with white handles popular in Druid and Wiccan traditions for making incisions, cutting herbs, or writing symbols on wood or wax.

The Book of Shadows: Shortened to "BOS," the renowned Gerald Gardner introduced this. The witch makes it with leather or a soft cloth for its cover and parchment or handmade paper for the pages. It is a book of rituals, chants, spells, beliefs, and ethics meant to guide a witch in practicing their craft. Traditionally, it existed in a single copy held by the High Priest or Priestess, but these days, other coven members have their own Book of Shadows, which must be destroyed upon an owner's death.

Cakes and Wine: Also called cakes and ale. This is a relaxed sharing of refreshments to end a ritual. The High Priest and Priestess must first sample the food before sharing it with the group.

Cantrip: A Scottish phrase for a minor magic spell. It could also refer to spells that read the same forward and backward.

Cauldron: An iron kettle or pot for burning fires, incense, preparing magical feasts, potions, and other supernatural brews. These days, witches use household pots that they consecrate for magic.

Censer: A small container for burning incense, herbs, and chemicals to purify the air, raise vibrational energies, and summon spirits before a ritual.

Chalice or Goblet: This represents the water element. It is used to hold sacrificial water or wine. When held upright, the chalice represents an open womb ready to contain or receive. An inverted chalice signifies rebirth and realization.

Circe: This is a Greek sorceress popular for her enchantments. She is famous for turning Odysseus's men into swine. In many tales, she is the daughter of Hecate, the patron Goddess of magic.

Cingulum: Latin for "belt" or "girdle." It's a consecrated witch's cord, usually nine feet in length. It's used to mark a sacred circle and is typically worn on the witch's waist like a karate belt to indicate their rank or initiation level.

Charm or Conjure Bags: These are drawstring pouches worn on the waist or neck containing magical objects of different kinds, from bones, sulfur, and salt, to nails, herbs, and gems. These bags are popular in voodoo practice.

Cookbook Witch: A witch who tries to teach herself magic using a book.

Coven: A group of Wiccans or witches, whose numbers range from three to twenty, though the traditional number is thirteen.

Cowan: The uninitiated, meaning anyone who isn't a Wiccan or witch.

Craft Name: A new name a witch receives following her initiation. Most craft names revolve around favorite deities.

Crossing the Bridge: A funeral.

Crown: A thin band of silver or gold with a crescent moon in front. Together with the cingulum, it conveys rank in a coven.

Degree (of Witchcraft): The four witchcraft degrees are a neophyte or first degree, middle stage or second degree, second-middle stage, and fully-fledged or third degree. Each degree has a unique symbol— an inverted triangle, a pentagram, and a triangle on top of a pentagram. Some witches write these symbols after their name.

Dedicant: One who devotes themselves to studying with a coven.

Deosil: Clockwise, in Gaelic orthography. It indicates a direction from East to West. It is known as the prosperous course and is the usual direction of a witch's spell casting, ritual circle, or dance.

Diana: Roman Goddess considered the Goddess of witches. Artemis is her Greek counterpart.

Drawing Down the Moon: An essential ritual in a Wiccan tradition where the High Priestess becomes the Goddess incarnate. It is performed on the first night of the full moon at the witching hour. *Drawing Down the Moon* is also a book written by Wiccan Priestess Margot Adler.

Drawing Down the Sun: A similar ritual to drawing down the moon, but for invoking the Horned God.

Elder: In some covens, you are an elder if you've led a coven for nine years.

Eostara: Pronounced with the "e" silent. Also called the Festival of Trees and Lady Day. This is celebrated on the Spring Equinox (March 21 in the Northern Hemisphere) and is one of the lesser Wiccan sabbats.

Esbat: A moon ritual to celebrate the Goddess and her energy. Twelve esbats coincide with twelve months of the year. Esbat could also mean a regular meeting of a coven. Its frequency depends on the coven.

Familiars: Low-ranking spirits in the form of animals that serve witches as spies, protectors, and companions. In witchcraft, cats are favored as familiars, as they are highly sensitive to psychic vibrations, negative energies, and power. This is why they are allowed in magic circles. In medieval times, African witches preferred owls, hyenas, baboons, and bats, while European witches liked dogs, cats, and toads.

Famtrad: Short for "family tradition." It's a Wiccan or witchcraft tradition revolving around the beliefs of a single-family instead of a coven.

Grimoire: Textbook of magic.

Halloween: Also called Samhain, or All Hallows' Eve. It acknowledges the fruits of the earth and the souls of the departed.

Handfasting: A Wiccan marriage ritual.

Hecate: The patron Goddess of witchcraft in Greek mythology. She is associated with knowledge of herbs, ghosts, necromancy, crossroads, sorcery, and night.

The Horned God: Cernunnos (Celtic), also known as Pan, Zeus, Thor, Adonis, or Hugh. He is depicted as a male goat or an object of lust.

Initiation: Rituals officially welcoming a budding witch into the coven after Wiccan studies.

Matrifocal: Female-focused.

Pentacle: An earth symbol. It is a star with five points, with one point pointing upwards, with a circle around it, which differentiates it from Satanism's pentagram. This is the most important symbol of witchcraft. Inverted pentacles without circles are often associated with the Church of Satan, and for this reason, Wiccans hardly use them in rituals to avoid that association.

Poppet or Puppet: Poppets are made of mud, cloth, silk, straw, wax, or wood, with bits of skin, nails, hair, and herbs. They are made for different reasons like a love spell, a protection spell, or a curse.

Rule of Three or Threefold Law: A tenet followed by Wiccans, occultists, and witches alike. The Law of Karma states:

Ever Mind the Rule of Three,

Three Times Your Acts Return to Thee.

This Lesson Well Thou Must Learn.

Thou Only Gets What Thee Dost Earn.

Sacred Circle: This is traditionally nine feet in circumference and drawn in the air using an athame. The circle has concentrated cosmic power and represents a realm between this world and the realm of the Gods.

Sabbat: Celebration of the Earth's journey around the Sun (the Wheel of the Year) through poetry, song, dance, and drama. There are eight sabbat rituals:

- Yule or Winter solstice (December 21 — N, June 21 — S).

- Imbolc or Candlemas (February 1 — N, August 1 — S).

- Ostara (Vernal equinox on March 21 — N, September 21 — S).

- Beltane (April 30 — N, October 31 — S).

- Litha (Summer solstice on June 21 — N, December 21 — S).

- Lughnasadh (August 1 — N, February 2 — S).

- Mabon (Autumn equinox on September 21 — N, March 21 — S).

- Samhain (October 31, both hemispheres).

Note that N = Northern hemisphere and S = Southern hemisphere.

Scrying: The art of looking into a medium (a black mirror, water bowl, or crystal ball) to receive visions or messages.

Self-Dedication: Personal ritual where a witch rededicates herself to the Goddess's service and that of her consort, the Horned God. It is done before an altar or with one's coven by sprinkling sea salt, lighting candles, and anointing the eyes, mouth, nose, breasts, loins, and feet with a mixture of water and wine.

Wand: A symbol of spiritual invocation. Wands represent the fire element and are plucked from tree branches in sacred groves. The best wands are formed from trees sacred to the Goddess, such as elderberry, mistletoe, oak, rowan, hazel, and willow. Wiccans inscribe a pentagram and their craft name on their wand, and then bless it using the Goddess's name. The strength of a wand is determined by the will of the witch who wields it.

Witching Hour: There is a lot of confusion as to when this is, but most consider it to be between 12 AM to 3 AM. It is the time when the barrier between this world and the world of the undead becomes thin, so that restless entities cross over seamlessly.

Wiccan Rede: A set of moral codes guiding Wiccans. The most popular is one promoting the use of magic with responsibility. It states:

"Do as ye will, an' it harm none."

Meaning: as long as your magic does not harm another, then it's okay.

Popular Misconceptions About Witches

If you asked anyone on the street what a witch is, they might say something along the lines of "bent-nosed women with pointy hats, broomsticks, familiars, boiling hot cauldrons, and spells." You can't blame them. Depictions of characters like the Wicked Witch of the West in the film *The Wizard of Oz* (1939) or the Grand High Witch in *The Witches* (1990) haven't helped. Below are a few false theories about witches and the truth behind them.

To Be a Witch, You Must Be Wiccan: This couldn't be further from the truth. Your ability to handle energy in the form of plants, herbs, rituals, spells, or reading the stars identifies you as a witch, regardless of the religion you are affiliated with. You also don't have to be from a line of witches to be one. This isn't a case of purebloods versus muggles.

Witches Are Women, While Warlocks and Wizards Are Men: Witchcraft is not gender-specific. Language is a fluid concept and prone to change. Anyone is free to brand themselves a witch, and no one has the right to judge the terms by which practitioners choose to label themselves. A warlock is a derogatory term used by witches to describe a male sorcerer who is a traitor, an outcast, or one who practices blood or dark magic.

Men and women have practiced magic for as long as we can recall, but women have paid the price for it with their lives. The stereotype of witches being female is likely a result of the fact that many of the people accused and executed for sorcery were female.

The Malleus Maleficarum, a Catholic treatise on witchcraft, accused women of being more vulnerable to devilish superstitions due to their innately jealous nature and malicious temperament. This is why, in many of the witchcraft traditions, women are regarded as superior to their male counterparts.

Witches Are Evil, Ride Brooms, and Eat Babies to Stay Young: This myth is a direct consequence of early Hollywood movies, religious fanaticism, and pop culture. People can be good or bad. So can witches. Evil is an innate character flaw. It has nothing to do with witchcraft.

Why go through the stress of killing a child when moisturizer and sunscreen have already been invented? Babies are cute to everyone, including witches. Witches have babies of their own, too. No, they don't eat salamander tails or the eyes of newts. They cook regular food and go to pizza parlors and salad bars, like everyone else.

Now, on to the idea that witches ride brooms. It's absurd, but here's why most people think that. Back in the Middle Ages, women made ointments out of ergot, a hallucinogenic fungus that grew on rye. They inserted them vaginally using broomsticks. They didn't fly—at least not literally. They only got high. There is also an old wives' tale about Pagan rituals involving witches who simulated flying on broomsticks to encourage high crop yield.

Witches Go Around Laying Curses and Hexes: Both are spells cast to cause harm to someone or something. The former does permanent damage, while the latter causes temporary harm. Magic may be a witch's medium for channeling their intentions into the world, but many Wiccan traditions abide by the Three-fold law or rule of three, which says that whatever magic you release into the world comes back to you threefold. This mindset helps witches practice their craft responsibly and, as such, avoid laying curses.

Being a Witch is Expensive: There is no need to drain your wallet or max out your credit card to become a witch. Many free Wiccan resources are available online. There are also online covens you can join at no extra cost. Some tools for your altar can be gotten at your dollar store. As you read more about witchcraft, you will find that "witchy" tools are all around you, from your pantry to your spice rack. But, if you have an extra dollar to spend on athames, crystals, wands, and the like, there are dedicated online shops for that.

All Witches Wear Black: There is no doubt that black is a beautiful color on its own, but many witches love a pop of color. They don't wear pointy hats. Some have fedoras and sunglasses, just as others love velvet capes and black fishnets, and others still would settle for a t-shirt and a comfy pair of jeans. Some even own fashion houses. And yes, while witches may love the idea of an owl delivery service, FedEx and DHL are more than enough for them.

Witches Worship the Devil and Own Black Cats: First, the devil is a Christian concept and has nothing to do with witchcraft. Some witches do worship Cernunnos, the Gaelic Horned God, which Puritans mistook as the devil. Witchcraft does not entail you selling your soul for magical powers.

As for black cats, the Druids and Celts loved them. They symbolize good luck, prosperity, love, and protection. Since the Christians launched a crusade against non-Christians, these cute felines were cast in a bad light. Puritans claimed the cats were witches in animal form. In the Middle Ages, cats were condemned by Pope Gregory IX and massacred by the Catholic Church. This led to a rat infestation and later the bubonic plague or "the black death," which was one of the most horrific plagues in human history.

Witchcraft Involves Memorizing Old Latin Verses for Spell Work: Memorizing incantations and blessings have their place in witchcraft, but it is not a prerequisite to becoming a full-fledged witch. Practiced rhymes and poems may have the ability to help you enter a transcendental state or connect to natural forces, but the real power of every spell is not the words but the strength and purity of intention.

To Be a True Witch, You Must Belong to a Coven: The word "coven" became popular in 1921 when Margaret Alice Murray popularized it, using it to describe a gathering of witches. Covens are great if you are into them, but witchcraft is a personal path. Witchcraft is a path to owning your power. Find what works for you and follow your gut. Fortunate enough to see a gathering that helps you grow as a witch? Then you might want to join them, and that's fine, but if you're a solitary witch who prefers to work alone, then practice as you see fit. It does not make you a greater or lesser witch.

The Lunar Phases and Their Significance to Witchcraft

Witches are in love with the moon and can harness the power of the lunar cycle for their spells. Witches think of the Sun as male energy and the moon as female energy or the Goddess's energy.

New Moon: This is the moon's primary phase and is also known as the crescent moon. It resembles the letter "D" or the right section of a parenthesis. It emphasizes a fresh start. Most times, the sky is dark, with the moon out of sight. It is the ideal time to identify our shadow selves or the parts of us we keep hidden. You can cast spells for letting go of your past, set new intentions for the forthcoming cycle, and let go of toxic people to make room for better ones.

Waxing Moon: The moon gradually increases in size, larger than the new moon, but not as big as the full moon. It's ideal for spells that encourage growth and advancement in your relationships, career, and just about any aspect of life. Want a new job or a raise? Or perhaps you want to renew the spark in a dull relationship? This phase is the perfect time to set those intentions.

Full Moon: This is the most powerful phase of the moon. Psychic powers and intuition are heightened, and the potency of all spells cast during this time is doubled. It is common for witches to charge their crystals or make moon water using this phase. Some witches combine the power of the full moon with sex magic. An intention set with an orgasm in the light of a full moon is going to work.

Waning Moon: Opposite of the waxing moon, the moon's brightness dims as it makes its way back to the new moon phase. This is ideal for getting rid of self-doubt, self-sabotaging behavior, unfair treatment, and insecurities. This is when you want to set intentions to get rid of all the things you no longer want to experience in life.

Dark Moon: This is typically not included in the four major phases and is often confused with the new moon. This phase lasts one to three days, depending on the Earth's position and distance from the Sun. The moon in this phase is not visible. It supports solitude, soul searching, and a period to cut you off from things and people you don't need, so you can find yourself and figure out what matters to you the most.

Intermediate or Secondary Phases of the Moon

Waning Crescent: The crescent moon grows dimmer and thinner until the light of the moon is gone.

Waxing Crescent: This happens after the dark moon. This phase is the first quarter of a waning moon and has a crescent sliver of the moon, less than a half-moon.

Waning Gibbous: Also called the third quarter. It happens after the full moon phase as moonlight continually reduces.

Waxing Gibbous: The moon's size increases and is more than half-full after the waxing crescent and first quarter.

Best Days for Moon Magic

Even with the lunar phases, certain days have energies suitable for certain forms of moon magic.

Sunday: Associated with the Sun, this day is suitable for matters concerning wellness, goals, career opportunities, agriculture, professional partnerships, civic issues, and mental health.

Monday: Associated with the moon, Mondays are full of feminine energy, and are the best days for increasing intuition and wisdom, past life regression, spiritual growth, healing medicine, culinary capabilities, and beauty.

Tuesday: Associated with Mars, Tuesday is full of masculine energy. It is a day for handling matters of a more physical nature such as fitness, physical and sexual stamina, protection rituals, issues involving law enforcement, and new beginnings. It is the best day for tests, surgeries, and adopting a pet.

Wednesday: Associated with the planet Mercury, Wednesday coincides with matters of the arts and communication, education, creativity, healing, and memory. This is the ideal day for outside the box thinking.

Thursday: Associated with Jupiter, this is the best day for religious and foreign pursuits, outdoor activities, luck, research, self-improvement, and mental and spiritual health. Sports competitions and wealth manifestations are the best today.

Friday: Associated with Venus, Friday's link to the Goddess of love is symbolic. This makes it a perfect day for love, pleasure, fertility, unions, and concentrating on relationships, music, dating, and self-expression. The waxing moon on a Friday is the perfect recipe to conjure up love or the perfect date. Little wonder that parties and get-togethers are on Fridays.

Saturday: Associated with Saturn, this is the day of transformation, protection, and spiritual cleansing. It is also the day to do away with habits, people, things, and thought processes harmful to you. For example, the waning moon on a Saturday is the perfect day to evict a troublesome tenant or a guest who has overstayed their welcome.

Chapter Four: Tools of the Craft

Tools and practices vary from tradition to tradition and from witch to witch. That being said, tools help harness magical energy, but they are optional. The most crucial tool for spell work is the caster's will, without which all other objects stay dormant. Below are a few tools you can start with. You don't need to have all of them. You can be resourceful during casting. Do not permit the lack of a tool to stop you from performing magic.

Beginner Magic Tools

Athamé or Athalmé: Pronounced a-tham-ay, this is a ritual blade symbolizing male energy, the element of fire, and, in some covens, the element of air. Called Yag-dirk by Saxons, it has a black hilt and is a double-edged blade, which is sometimes crescent-shaped to represent the moon. It is used to direct magical energy, cast ritual circles, banish negative energies, and conduct invocation rituals. It is not a cutting tool, and it can be engraved with runes or sigils. Some hereditary witches believe athames should never be made of metal as it interrupts with earth energy. For this reason, traditional witches make athames from flint.

Bells: These are common in Pagan traditions. A bell's body is reminiscent of the ancient images of human genitalia; the handle represents the phallus and the body a vulva. Other symbologists claim the bell's body represents the womb and the handle the child within. For this reason, most Wiccan bells are shaped to resemble the figure of a woman.

Witches use smaller bells with handles for removing the evil eye, summoning or banishing entities, performing cleansing rituals, facilitating healing processes, and empowering fertility spells. Bells hung on surfaces or entrances serve as protective amulets or magical guard dogs warning against evil spirits. Some sects drink potions from the bell's cup-shaped portion, as it's believed to add potency to herbal brews.

Bolline: A knife used for cutting during spell work and magical rituals. Traditionally it is double-edged and white-handled, in contrast to the athame. Think of the bolline as a practical knife and the athame as a ceremonial knife. The different colors of the handles allow for easy identification and prevent one from desecrating the athame. You can use a standard knife as a bolline. Bollines are used in chopping herbs, carving inscriptions, cutting fabric, thread, or cords.

Besom or Broomstick: One of the staple altar tools in witchcraft. It represents male and female energies. The stick is the male force inserted into the female twigs or straw. Witchcraft has been linked to brooms for ages, with the popular misconception that they served as transportation devices. Brooms serve as a tool for crossing from one realm to the next and sweep an area clean of energetic and physical debris.

They are also used to sweep away footprints, as footprints left behind are vulnerable to evil magic. Anyone who wishes to harm you can do so using footprints you have left behind. Brooms are one of the sacred attributes of Hecate, and today, they have become a symbol of witchcraft, brazenly displayed by Wiccans in memory of the burning times. They are easily made, although there are beautiful ones sold in online craft shops like Etsy. The traditional besom has an ash handle, willow bindings, and a birch brush, but you should use tools available to you, like everything else.

Book of Shadows: A book of magical texts and instructions used in many Pagan religions, and Wicca as well, for taking notes of spells, rituals, and other invocations.

Burine: Not to be confused with the diuretic pill, this is a sharp tool used by witches to carve symbols, words, or designs into supernatural objects. Burines can be nails, pins, or crystal points.

Candles and Incense: These are an essential aspect of witchcraft and have an entire field dedicated to their study. Both are inexpensive, easy to find, and are convenient for witches in the closet to practice openly.

Compass: Many rituals and energy alignment practices involve the four cardinal directions, and the witch who isn't spatially aware needs a compass to orient correctly.

Crystals: These serve as both psychic materials and tools. Different crystals are associated with different powers and elements. They are used for many rituals, from creating a sacred circle to cleansing and charging other magical tools, to helping you get and stay in the zone during spell work.

Cards: These are popular divination and spell casting tools. There are different cards for divination, meditation, and other uses, but tarot cards are the most popular divination cards. In medieval times, Christians called them the devil's picture book and saw their presence in a home as sin. Invented in East Asia, there is still some controversy about whether these cards are Chinese or Korean in origin. Tarot suits correspond to various magical tools like the pentacle, chalice, and so on. The earliest surviving tarot deck is the Visconti-Sforza deck.

Cauldrons: The word "cauldron" originates from the Latin "caldarium," meaning "hot bath." it represents the water element and female energy and also signifies the universal womb and resurrection. In ancient Egyptian hieroglyphics, the symbol of a woman was a pot. The most famous cauldron in history is the gilded silver Gunderstrup Cauldron of 1891, now kept at the National Museum of Copenhagen.

Cauldrons are used in spell work for brewing potions, containing fire, burning candles, cooking food, making medicine, and conducting harmful magic. For instance, covering a poppet with one signifies entombing an enemy. Traditionally, cast iron is the metal of choice, but other materials such as ceramic, porcelain, brass, and copper can be used as well. Protect your pot from rust by coating it with grease or oil and heating it at 375 degrees Fahrenheit for one hour. If your cauldron is rusty, you can use the Coca-Cola trick. Pour some into the pot and leave overnight. Wash it off using steel wool the next day.

Chalice or Goblet: A drinking cup or vessel corresponding to the water element, this is a symbol of feminine energy or the womb of the Goddess and is typically made of silver to represent lunar energy. The most famous chalice is the Holy Grail. Sharing a chalice during rites with coveners shows unity and connectedness of purpose. Chalices are also formed from indigo glass or crystal. The Great Wiccan Rite is celebrated by dipping an athame into a chalice.

Cords: Cords and knots have many magical uses. Small cords are used in knot spells to manifest a desire, command, or wish. Knots are also used for sex, love, protection, healing, and hexing spells. The long cord or cingulum is tied in nine knots, and it is in these knots that the cingulum's power resides. Braided together, they can be used in binding rituals, for casting sacred circles, forging weather spells, and measuring a coven circle's circumference.

Crystal Ball: This has been used since the early 19th century by fortunetellers and witches as a potent divination tool. It is not as common today, but it's still as relevant in witchcraft. It's a round globe formed from a crystal, and it comes in different colors. It is associated with water and femininity. It is also used in spirit summoning and shamanic communication. A fine crystal ball is an expensive investment, so for this reason, they are not as popular as tarot cards. When not in use, crystal balls are covered with a cloth or kept in an opaque box and cleaned using magical washes, incense smoke, and herbal flower-infused spring water.

Horns and Cornucopias: These are kept on the altar and used for summoning spirits. Some Wiccan sects use the horn as a chalice during rituals, and it can be attached to caps during festivities when a High Priest imitates the Horned God.

Masks: Made from crystals, wood, clay, fabric, hemp, feathers, leather, stone, papier mâché, and a variety of materials, they serve as ceremonial portals permitting the wearer entry into a magical realm. They also offer protection from evil forces, act as shields or talismans, and receptacles of a divine force. Masks are used in covering the faces of the deceased and serve as votive offerings. In the medieval era, witches wore full or half masks to maintain anonymity and prevent capture.

Mirrors: Today's mirrors are made from glass. Ancient mirrors were crafted from copper that was polished until it became reflective. Mirrors are used in protective spells, love magic, scrying, and spirit summoning. They are associated with deities like Oshun, Venus, and Hathor and are prevalent in many religions, popularly Aztec, Celtic, and folk magic.

Mortar and Pestle: Once referred to as a witchy transportation device, the mortar and pestle are old primal grinding tools. In witchcraft, they are used in crushing herbs and making ointments for various purposes. Modern tools can be used for the same purpose, but the mortar and pestle is symbolic because it puts you in touch with your spell materials and desired intentions in a way that the touch of a button cannot imitate. The molcajete and tejolote made from volcanic rock are the traditional Mexican mortar and pestle for witches. Today, they are fashioned from glass, marble, brass, stone, and terracotta.

Pentacle: A fundamental Wiccan tool representing the earth element. The pentacle serves as an emblem, protective amulet, or talisman, like the cross is for Christians and the hexagram for the Jews. The earliest pentacle dates back to 4000 CE.

Singing Bowls: An alloy of seven metals (gold, antimony, copper, mercury, silver, iron, and tin) kept on an altar to attract harmonious cosmic energy in the form of sound, to purify a space, attune the chakras, and help in astral travel and spellwork.

Stang: A two-pronged wooden staff used in Wiccan rituals. The word "stang" is an old Norse word meaning pole or staff. The bifurcations on the stang represent the horns of the Horned God. Stangs are used in casting spells and calling spirits. They also serve as a compass when placed north of a sacred circle and as a magical focal point to direct energy. You can make your own at home using a branch from elm, ash, magnolia, and a carving knife.

Wand: This corresponds to the fire element and is traditionally six inches long, though you can adjust its length for your comfort. Early wands were wooden and cut from the yew, willow, rowan, or oak trees. Hazel is the best wood for wand making, followed by ash rowan or willow cut during the waxing or full moon. These days, wands can be made of glass or metal and adorned with gemstones. They are used in drawing up or directing energy. Unlike the *Harry Potter* franchise, you choose your wand. You'll feel it in your gut when you have found the right one. Yet, your wand remains a rod until you fill it with power and intention.

Feel free to create your own tools if you have carpentry or metal forging skills. If you choose to buy one, ask about its history and make sure it hasn't been defiled by blood.

Cleaning and Storing Magical Tools

Tools and crystals are purified with holy water made from mixing spring water and sea salt under a full moon. Crystals, like other magic tools, absorb energy, thoughts, and emotions for a long time. There are a variety of ways to clean them.

- Use running water and mild soap.

- Energetically clean them by rubbing them with a piece of citrine.

- Leave them in moonlight or sunlight for a short time.

- Bury them in a dish of brown rice or dirt.

- Soak them in seawater or saltwater.

- Purify using incense or smudge with white sage.

Each time you use a tool for a magical purpose, it is necessary to clean it. Also, purify your tools if someone else handles them. This way, the energy of another does not interfere with your spells. While cleaning, envision a white light flowing through them.

Like any prized heirloom, you want to protect your tools by storing them carefully. You can choose to display them on an altar, as long as it is out of sight to prevent others from touching the items. Keep tools wrapped in velvet pouches or silk, and store them in cupboards, boxes, closets, or trunks to protect them from contamination by dust, direct light, and energy vibrations.

Charging Tools and Crystals

Charging is the process of dedicating and consecrating tools for your purposes, transforming simple objects into elements of magic. You can charge in the following ways:

Using the Four Elements: Sprinkle some ocean water or water with sea salt on your tools and say, "With earth and water, I bid you do my will." Light a candle or some incense and hold it in the smoke for a few seconds, saying, "With fire and air, I bid you do my will." Ensure you wipe down your tools after sprinkling them with salt water to prevent corrosion.

Charging with Essential Oils: It is common to charge your tools with a single essential oil or an oil blend. When doing this, say, "With this oil, I bid you do my will." Wands may be charged with sandalwood, cinnamon, patchouli, clove, or musk oil; athames with lavender, ginger, honeysuckle, and carnation; chalices with ylang-ylang, jasmine, or rose; and pentagrams with pine, fennel, mint, basil, or anise. You may decide to make your oil blends or have a personal charging ritual. That's okay. There is no right or wrong way to do magic. Work with your intuition to make your tools work for you.

You can also charge using reiki, moon water, sunlight, total eclipses, herbs, seawater, crystals, and sound (with a singing bowl). Always have at least three decks of cards: one for personal divination, one for divining for others, and the third for spell work. Guarantee that magical tools are used for magical purposes only. Once you treat your tools with respect, they will serve you for the rest of your life.

Popular Magical Herbs and Their Uses

- **Allspice:** Prosperity, healing, love, good luck, energy.

- **Angelica:** Protection and purification.

- **Basil:** Success, protection, tranquility, love, and peace.

- **Bay:** Wisdom, success, divination, and prophetic dreams.

- **Calendula and Chamomile:** Love, prosperity, harmony, increase in psychic powers, and happiness.

- **Caraway and Clove:** Protection.

- **Cinnamon:** Money, success, love, purification, and vitality.

- **Comfrey:** Safety during journeys, prosperity.

- **Dill:** Good fortune, protection, passion, tranquility.

- **Ginger:** Energy booster and increases the likelihood of success and financial independence.

- **Marjoram:** Protection, joy, happiness, love.

- **Mint:** Love, fertility, joy, prosperity, purification.

- **Mugwort:** Protection, consecration, relaxation, banishing.

- **Nutmeg:** Happiness, love, psychic ability booster, abundance.

- **Parsley:** Prosperity, purification, strength, and passion.

- **Rosemary:** Memory booster, increases wisdom, and provides protection.

- **Sage:** Purification, protection, longevity, wisdom, and health.

- **Verbena:** Protection, inspiration, healing, a reversal of negativity, creativity booster.

- **Yarrow:** Also called bloodwort. Useful for love, courage, and healing.

Some lesser-known plants used in magic include:

- **Moss:** Perseverance, tenacity, patience, toughness.

- **Ferns:** Collect these before midnight on the eve of the summer solstice to help in invisibility. No, we're not talking about literal invisibility. It allows you to go about your tasks without getting noticed.

- **Grass:** Its adaptability makes it ideal for spells that improve the flexibility of thought and surrender to fate.

Popular Magical Trees

- **Apple:** Cutting an apple in half shows a seed arrangement similar to the shape of a pentagram. That is proof of its magical power. It is used in fertility, longevity, love, creativity, and abundance spells.

- **Ash:** This is associated with strength, wisdom, willpower, justice, protection, skill, travel, and water.

- **Birch:** The traditional besom is made from twigs of the birch tree. Early cradles were made with birchwood. This tree is associated with purification and protection.

- **Cedar:** This is used for spirituality, healing, harmony, prosperity, and purification.

- **Elder:** Also called witchwood, legend has it that bad luck follows anyone who doesn't ask its permission thrice before harvesting any part of it. Elder wood is associated with the Goddess of incarnation and is used for protection (particularly against lightning), healing, and prosperity.

- **Hawthorn:** Also called mayflower or may tree, it is connected to happiness, fertility, harmony, protection, and otherworldly realms.

- **Hazel:** This grants protection, wishes, luck, and fertility.

- **Honeysuckle:** Also called a hedge tree or woodbine, it is great for happiness, healing, prosperity, and psychic awareness.

- **Maple:** This offers prosperity, love, health, and abundance.

- **Oak:** A Druid favorite; it promotes longevity, courage, protection, good fortune, and strength.

- **Pine:** This is great for purification, protection, healing, prosperity, and clearing the mind. Amber, a gem renowned for luck and harmony of energy centers, is made from fossilized pinesap.

- **Poplar:** Also called aspen, it is associated with exorcisms, prosperity, communication, and purification.

- **Rowan:** Also known as mountain ash, it is a witch's favorite for divination, protection, creativity, success, boosting psychic powers, and transformation.

- **Willow:** Associated with the Goddess, it is used for increasing intuition, harmony, love, healing, renewal, protection, and growth.

- **Witch Hazel:** This promotes healing, peace, and protection.

- **Yew:** Its poisonous nature is why it is always associated with death, the otherworld, and spirits.

When doing tree magic, fresh woods contain a lot of living energy, which is beneficial in rituals and spells. Deadfall is wood discarded by the tree and does not contain vibrant energy. The spell you choose to cast will determine the type and nature of wood you require. If you decide to use fresh wood, it is advised that you ask the tree, plant, or bush for permission and take what you need with respect and care. If you can, leave an offering for the tree as appreciation.

Useful Apps for the Budding Witch

Thanks to the increase in spirituality and the rising popularity of witchcraft, there are lots of apps available that can help you to practice your craft on the go.

- **Tarot Mastery:** Labyrinthos, Spirit Animal Oracle Cards App, Golden Thread Tarot, Luminous Spirit Tarot, Classic Rider-Waite Tarot App.

- **Lunar Calendar and Wicca Holidays:** My Moon Phase, Daff Moon, Wicca Calendar, Cosmic Watch (iPhone), Natal Charts with Transits, SkyView Free.

- **Mindfulness and Meditation:** Insight Timer, Ike, and Headspace.

- **Books on Witchcraft:** Audible, Kindle, Scribd.

- **Spell Writing:** Notebook.

- **Herbology:** About Herbs, PlantNet, Wicca Herbarium.

- **Divination and Astrology:** Co-Star, Rune App.

- **Wiccan Communities:** Witches and Witchcraft Amino.

- **Crystal Mastery:** Stone (iPhone), Crystals Light App.

- **Runes, Newsletters, and Spells:** Spellcaster.

- **Candle App for Spells and Meditation:** SoonSoon Candle App.

- **Horoscopes:** SunSigns.

Chapter Five: Building Your Altar

From the beginning of time, humans have always had designated spaces. There is a space for cooking, one for bathing and another for sleeping. It only makes sense that you would have a special area for worship as a witch who takes their craft seriously, right?

Altars can be big or small, a room or a tiny corner. You don't need an elaborate set-up or a castle with moats and high towers. The size of your accommodation will determine if you have somewhere you can dedicate to your craft: or you can go "porta-witch," by carrying your altar around with you. Many people may argue that since God and the Goddess live in all things, then everywhere is an altar. That is true, technically. But, as a witch, you would agree that your altar should be a place that is extra sacred, free of evil energies, and consecrated for a specific purpose—witchcraft.

Sacred Circles Versus Altars

Sacred or magic circles have been used in ancient ceremonial and Babylonian magic. They represent areas of non-physical space, a microcosm or psychic bubble constructed with power and intent. Such intentions include protection from evil forces and communication with deities. Sacred circles may be marked out physically using chalk, salt, cord, ash, or sulfur.

Wiccan circles are traditionally nine feet in diameter, although this may vary depending on the caster's preference, the circle's purpose, and available space. Many elaborate patterns for sacred circles exist in grimoires and magic manuals, mostly involving angels and other celestial beings.

An altar is set up within a sacred circle. Altars are elevated sacred spaces used by witches for spell work and communing with the Gods. They come in an array of shapes and sizes. There is no one way it should look. You can use a coffee table or a nice round table from the home development section in IKEA. Some people use fireplaces, hearths, or the side of a chimney as an altar. You can also have an outdoor altar in the form of a flat stone, tree stump, or a flat expanse of land with a stang as the focus and other artifacts arranged around it. After all, what better way to communicate with the spirits than outside in nature?

You have to exercise caution with outdoor altars. You don't want to get picked up by the police while performing a banishing spell with your athame in hand, dressed in your robe with a cape. Not a very pretty picture, to be honest. For this reason, many witches prefer indoor altars. When fashioning your altar, it should be made of non-conductive materials like wood, stone, brass, silver, or gold. Only magical tools like the athame should be made of conductive materials. Most purposeful altars are fashioned from willow, a tree sacred to the Goddess. A square altar represents the four elements, while a round one represents the moon, the Goddess, and spirituality.

Altar Location

Traditional witches prefer to set up permanent altars in the north or east, so their movements are oriented in such directions. When placed in the north, they attract success and prosperity. In the south, they work great for career and finance. Toward the east, it promotes health and longevity. To the west, it boosts creativity. Set it in the northeast for spirituality, the southeast for change, the northwest for partnerships and relationships, and the southwest for support. If you need a fresh start, your altar should face east where the sun rises because the rising sun marks new beginnings each day.

If your allocated space does not allow for such set-ups, then place your altar wherever you wish to, bearing in mind that your space must make you feel safe and loved. If you decide to keep your altar away from prying eyes, you can either keep it in a room under lock and key or disguise it, so it seems like you have an eclectic sense of interior design. Its location depends on your magical intentions and the God or Goddess you honor. If you seek abundance, light, comfort, and security, an altar in your dining hall or kitchen is advised. Guidance in romantic matters or in honor of Aphrodite may be placed near a bathroom vanity or in a bedroom. Different cardinal directions represent a specific aspect of life.

Cleansing the Space for Your Altar

Once you have decided on the location, the next thing is to clean your altar physically and energetically. Physically, clean with a broom and cleaning supplies. You could invest in a gentle sea-salt based detergent for this purpose. Perform psychic cleansing by smudging with white sage, tobacco, sweetgrass, or cedar. This gets rid of psychic debris and re-energizes the space for new beginnings. To smudge your altar using the four elements, I would recommend the following:

- **A Suitable Herb:** The most popular are white sage, palo-santo, cedar, sweetgrass, pine, lemongrass, juniper, and lavender. Since most herbs like sage and palo-santo suffer from over-harvesting, I recommend you purchase ethically sourced herbs from honest, reputable, environmentally conscious shops or sites. The herbs you burn represent the earth element, while the smoke represents the air.

- **A Smudge Pot:** This is made of ceramic, metal, or stone. It represents the element of water. You can use an abalone shell to catch the ash. Try not to expose abalone shells to direct heat since they can get scorched. You may use a wooden stand to hold the smudge pot steady and elevate it to prevent your altar from suffering direct heat.

- **A Source of Fire:** Lighter, matches, or flint (for purists).

- **Feathers or Fans:** These represent the air element. Purists use turkey feathers or hand-painted eagle feathers. This is optional, as you can tie a yellow ribbon around your smudge stick (yellow is the color for air) and wave it around or use your hands to spread the smoke.

- **Drums or Sacred Drumming Music:** This sound represents the heartbeat. You can also use pre-recorded shamanic or Native American drum music. No drums or music? No problem! Listen to your heartbeat or set an intention for music, trusting spirit to do the work for you.

While smudging, you can say, "With this (name of herb), I cleanse my tools and dispel any negative energy from this space, so they are used for my greatest benefit," or "Air, fire, water, earth; purify, dismiss, and dispel."

Once you finish cleansing your space, you can let the herbs burn out, extinguish them with sea salt, or smother the flames yourself. End with a short blessing like: "I dedicate this space to (name of deity). May it be a place of joy, upliftment, and spiritual growth."

To Decorate or Not to Decorate?

There are no right or wrong items to use when building your sacred space. Several texts spell out objects that should be on your altar, like there is some rulebook that states what should and what shouldn't be there. This book aims to change that narrative.

The first thing to keep in mind is that your choice is key when it comes to your altar. It should reflect your intentions and tastes. You can keep a bunch of stuff, or opt for a minimalist design, or you could change décor according to the seasons, or have a striking décor for your birthday. It's all up to you.

When building your altar, it is recommended that you create an aura of balance and harmony by placing objects that signify the four elements and cardinal points.

- A bowl of clean water or a mirror represents the west and the water element.

- A bowl of earth, salt, or a crystal for the north and earth element.

- Some feathers, lit incense sticks, a wind chime, a fan, or athame for east and the air element.

- Lit candles, incense for the fire element, and south.

- Masks, cloth dolls, or crystals with ancient Sumerian symbols for heaven, sky, and spirit.

Add an offering tray containing your intentions, like a key if you desire a house, a car figurine if you want a car or coins for extra income. Represent the sky that covers all other elements by using celestial or heavenly symbols or pictures.

Use crystals and gems as focal points for manifesting intentions in your rituals and spells. Trust your intuition and don't rush when picking crystals for this purpose.

Select crystals according to themes. For example, Black Tourmaline, Obsidian, Malachite, Hematite, and Agate are great for protection; Charoite, Celestite, Labradorite, Sugilite, and Angelite boost psychic abilities; Jade, Aventurine, Moonstone, and Clear Quartz promote harmony and balance. Crystals amplify your intentions. When used with herbs, essential oils, and incense, they clear away bad energies, improve your mood, and ground you, thus setting the mood for magic.

You will need your Book of Shadows, grimoire, or magic journal. In this, you write down your spells, notes, recipes, and rituals by hand. You can also pen down the lunar cycle and corresponding sabbats. Never use your journal for any mundane purposes. Leave it permanently on the altar if need be.

If you wish, you may pick a deity or spirit to work with. This is entirely optional and dependent on what you want to achieve. For instance, Lord Ganesh, Goddess Lakshmi, or the laughing Buddha are deities synonymous with abundance, money spells, and wealth. Build an altar in memory of beloved relatives who have crossed over by placing pictures, food items, or objects they valued on it. Even a hairbrush or a cup of coffee made the way they like would do, as long as it is what they desire. Just make sure it's clean. When working with deities or spirits, please research offerings suitable for them.

Many witches choose to decorate their altar with an altar cloth. You can buy one or make one yourself. Crochet or sew patterns that mean something to you. You may even use a plain tablecloth onto which you can sew runes and reiki symbols if you want to.

Traditional Wiccan altar cloths are made from natural and sustainable materials like wool, cotton, silk, linen, and so on. If you must use altar cloths, you could color coordinate them with the spell's intentions. For instance, green signifies fertility, abundance, and the Earth mother; black is for protection, wisdom, and self-defense; and silver is for dreams, psychic connections, astral projection, and telepathy.

The left side of the altar is typically ascribed to the Goddess. Place tools synonymous with her such as the pentacle, chalice, cauldron, wand, bells, crystals, and besom. You may also include pictures or figurines of the Earth mother if you have them. In their absence, a green or silver candle may suffice. If your altar is dedicated to the triple Goddess, you may use three candles to honor her as the Mother (white), Maiden (red), and Crone (black).

The altar's right side is ascribed to the Horned God. Keep objects synonymous with him such as the athame, Book of Shadows, censer, bolline, and sword here. You can add a figurine or deity of the Horned God. If you don't have this, then a gold candle might suffice. If you intend to work magic, make sure that all your tools (candles, journal, pen, written or printed inspirations like words of affirmation or a poem, herbs, oils, lighter, and so on) are placed on or beneath the altar. You can incorporate refreshments to use as ritual offerings or for replenishing energy spent while working. Feel free to add totems of your favorite or spirit animal, pictures of your pet, and other artifacts that get you in the zone.

If for any reason you need to leave the circle around your altar, using anti-clockwise motions, cut open a doorway with the athame in your dominant hand while facing northeast. Ask a fellow witch to stand guard for you at the door or if you are practicing alone, place your broomstick at the doorway to dispel negative forces. When you return, don't forget to close the circle using a clockwise motion.

Flower Power for Your Altar

If you are using flowers on your altar, below are a few that witches commonly use and their significance.

- **Carnation:** Strength, healing, energy, luck, and protection.

- **Daffodil, Tulip, Poppy:** Fertility, abundance, love, success, and luck.

- **Daisy, Gardenia, Hyacinth:** Flirtation, love, and protection.

- **Geranium, Snapdragon, Lilac:** Protection.

- **Jasmine:** Seduction and sensuality.

- **Lavender, Rose, Violet:** Harmony, peace.

- **Lily, Pansy:** Happiness, communication.

Your altar, like your craft, is continuously evolving. Your intentions may change, and you might need to make a few adjustments to the items on the altar as this happens. Who knows? You might need more than one altar for different purposes. Just let spirit lead.

Tending to Your Altar

Your altar is not only holy, it is swirling with living energy. Would you want to visit someone and be left on the doorstep or ignored? This is why giving some TLC to your sacred space, and "feeding" it keeps your intentions fresh and prevents stagnant energy. Here are a few tips to consider in caring for your altar:

1. Anoint deities or statues.

2. If you have flowers, change them as often as possible and clean out the vase so the water stays fresh.

3. Light new candles and clean out the wax from the old ones.

4. If you are a neat freak, then purchase Himalayan salt lamps or selenite lamps.

5. Burn candles regularly and light incense with scents that resonate with your intention or preferred deity.

6. Sweep the area around your altar regularly, wash altar cloths, clear cobwebs if any, and wipe down statues if you anoint them with oils.

7. Charge your crystals under the light of the full moon every month.

8. If you own a singing bowl, rattle it at least twice a week to raise cosmic energies around the altar.

9. Change offerings regularly. Offerings could be coins, shells, flowers, herbs, or other items.

10. Meditate daily in your temple, sing, chant, dance, and reaffirm the intentions set for your altar or create new ones if the need arises.

11. Give thanks and show gratitude. You could do this by baking goods infused with herbs that your deity prefers, or saying a simple "thank you" over and over again.

Rituals for the Budding Witch

Rituals are at the heart of witchcraft. A ritual is a ceremony or rite performed for a specific purpose. Some are formal with structure and certain rules, while others are loosely planned and guided solely by intuition. Some rituals that could be conducted by witches at their altars include:

- **Hallowing or Consecration Ritual:** This is done to consecrate a tool and imbue it with magical powers and is best performed during the full or waxing moon.

- **Purification Ritual:** This ritual helps you rid yourself, your space, and your tools of all that is negative and unclean. It is done before performing a magic spell. Initial purification rituals are best conducted on the night of the new moon.

- **Banishing Rituals:** These help to rid a place, person, or tool of baneful entities and stagnant energies. Perform as regularly as possible.

- **Invocation Rituals:** These involve casting a magic circle to draw the energy of a deity or higher power into oneself.

- **Treading the Mill Ritual:** A traditional ritual done to heighten spiritual awareness and magical powers. This involves continuously pacing about a compass while keeping the eyes fixed on a spiritual focal point, such as a stang or flame.

The witch paces with the head cocked to one side and slightly tilted backward. This restricts some blood flow to the brain, and in addition to the fixation on a particular object, induces a trance-like state—essential for working magic. This ritual is preferably performed on an outdoor altar; though, there have been witches that have been resourceful enough to "tread the mill" indoors.

- **Cakes and Ale or Cakes and Wine Ritual:** The serving of refreshments done to conclude any ritual. Serve cakes from a pentacle plate and wine from a cup or chalice. "Cakes" could be cookies, fruit, crackers, or any grain-based meal. "Wine" could be juice, ale, or water.

Chapter Six: Keeping a Grimoire or Book of Shadows

The Origin of The Book of Shadows

If modern witchcraft were a human entity, its parents would be Gerald Brosseau Gardner and Doreen Edith Valiente. Before meeting Valiente, Gardner came across fragments of a manuscript he claimed was written by a group of European witches. He wrote down several practices and rituals from the study of Western and Eastern esoteric philosophy, namely Celtic folklore, Tantric yoga, Aleister Crowley's work, and Enochian wisdom.

Valiente edited the material discarding many of Crowley's texts while adding poetry and some information of her own. The result became an essential guide for practitioners of Gardnerian Wicca. This manuscript wasn't originally called a Book of Shadows. It was called *Ye Bok of Ye Art Magical.*

The name changed when Gardner came across a 1949 edition of *The Occult Observer* magazine in Brighton, England, containing an article on a Sanskrit manuscript titled *Book of Shadows*, written by an Indian palmist Mia Bashir. The article appeared opposite *High*

Magic's Aid, a fantasy witchcraft novel written by him. He decided to use this title, which is significant for witches today.

The Grimoire and Its History

The early definition of a grimoire called it a book of magic, spells, invocations, incantations, evocations, and a host of other practices used to call upon spirits. Grimoires have existed in ancient Babylonia, Middle Eastern civilizations, and medieval Renaissance times. Grimoires were associated with any one of the three major world religions—Christianity, Islam, and Judaism—and impacted early science and the arts in Europe and part of Asia. Hence, as much as many forbid them, they are essential aspects of our cultural history.

Grimoire, pronounced "grim-wahr," originates from Middle English "gramere" and Old French "grammaire," which refers to language and spelling rules. The root word is translated from the Latin "grammatical" and Greek "grammatikos," meaning: "of letters or grammar." Its origins from pantheistic civilizations are probably why it's a text dedicated to rites that honor the Goddess.

Grimoires were once illegal. The Archbishop of Paris ordered the destruction of texts, booklets, and scrolls on sorcery, demonic conjuration, and necromancy in 1277. These weren't just textbooks of spells and magic rituals; they were expressly forbidden. If caught with a magical text in medieval times, the punishment was severe. You were tortured until you confessed under pain. After this, you were burned alive with the text at your feet, so you never forgot what caused you the trouble in the first place.

Still, regardless of the numbers sacrificed for these taboo texts, more have been willing to die to possess the knowledge within. For this reason, fragments of individual texts and their forgeries have been preserved, recreated, and circulated again and again.

Magic texts were written in obscure texts and foreign languages, some in several languages at once. This added to the air of mystery, as most of the population was illiterate. These hassles never stopped anyone from copying and attempting to translate them. Whether these texts were authentic or not, we will never know. There was no one to ask. Inquiring from someone puts you at risk of arrest and torture by inquisitors.

Grimoires, as we know them, started appearing in the 12th century, most with no known and sometimes dead authors. No one in the Middle Ages wanted to take credit for writing grimoires. They were always given or "found" by mysterious strangers. These medieval texts had new editions made by manually copying old ones at great risk.

Grimoires contained inspiration from many sources, which included but was not limited to:

- Jewish angelology and Kabbalistic texts.

- Roman Catholic practices like exorcism rituals.

- Egyptian magical papyri.

- Alchemical mysteries and rituals.

- Pagan texts of magic from Rome, Greece, and the Byzantine Empire.

Famous Ancient Grimoires

Since the beginning of time, mystics and magicians alike have compiled writings of their art. Many are lost or missing mainly because the Church saw them as sinful. Some still exist, and today, provide some insight into the magic done by our ancestors. Below are a few famous grimoires:

1. The Grand Grimoire or Red Dragon: Written in French around the mid-17th century, it is a text of necromancy and demonic conjuring and one of the evilest books ever written. One of the demons conjured is Lucifuge Rofocale, a treasure-hunting demon. Summoning this entity is only advised when you can escape making a pact with it. Legend has it that it claims your soul after 20 years of service.

2. The Great Albert by Albert Magnus: The full title of this grimoire is *Albertus Magnus, Being the Approved, Verified, Sympathetic and Natural Egyptian Secrets or White and Black Art for Man and Beast Revealing the Forbidden Knowledge and Mysteries of Ancient Philosophers.* The earliest German manuscript was written in 1478. It is a book of medicine and mysticism, with strong Christian foundations.

3. Grimoire of Honorius the Great: Written by Pope Honorius III before his death in 1227, this is a magic text with Christian orientations, supposedly for Christian sorcerers. It contains spells for summoning, dismissing, commanding, and binding demons, as well as animal sacrifices, prayers, and instructions on how to create a magical book.

4. Clavicula Salomonis (Keys of Solomon) and the Lemegeton (Lesser Key of Solomon): These texts inspired all medieval grimoires. They were written in Greek by King Solomon, the world's most powerful mystic, and believed to have existed with fragments found since the 4th century. The oldest surviving copy lies in the British Museum and contains ancient ceremonial Jewish magic to control and summon spirits. It also includes rituals on animal sacrifice. *The Grand Grimoire* contains some information from the *Clavicula Salomonis.*

5. Munich Manual of Demonic Magic (15th Century): Also called *Liber Incantationum, Exorcismorum et Fascinationum,* it is written in Latin with Roman Catholic rituals for invisibility, summoning, and banishing demons using sacred circles and words of power.

6. Picatrix (Ghayat al-Hakim — The Goal of the Wise): Written in Arabic in Andalusia by mathematician al-Majriti in 1000 CE when Spain was under Islamic rule, this is a compilation of four books of astral, talismanic, and sympathetic magic, grounded in classical Arabian magic, with reference to Hermes Trismegistus. It contains spells for healing, love, longevity, control over, and escape from enemies. The largest and rarest grimoire to exist, it was translated into Latin for King Alfonso the Wise in 1256.

7. The Sacred Book of Abra-Melin the Mage: This is one of the most powerful and complete magic grimoires. Described by Crowley as the best and most dangerous book to exist, it was initially written in 1458 by Abraham of Worms for his son Lamech. Abraham gained the knowledge from an Egyptian mage and Kabbalah master called Abra-Melin. Twelve manuscripts exist, each one in a different language.

8. The Sixth and Seventh Books of Moses: These controversial texts contain incantations for summoning, banishing, and commanding spirits. Later texts contain secret fears of Vatican and Jewish conspiracies. Allegedly revealed to Moses on Mount Sinai, then passed from generation to generation until King Solomon used it to invoke spirits, it is written in a combination of mixed Hebrew, Latin, and German. The sixth book contains magic seals, and the seventh, magic tables.

9. Leland's Grimoire or Aradia, the Gospel of the Witches: American folklorist Charles Godfrey wrote this at the end of the 19th century. One of the first English grimoires that strongly influenced neo-Paganism and Wicca, it has claims of magic lore given by a mysterious witch named Maddalena, who is said to have received knowledge from an ancient group of Goddess worshippers.

Many historic grimoires are in private collections and national museums like the Arsenal Library (Paris) and British Museum (London), with some expensive (albeit dubious) books masquerading as the original, occasionally showing up for sale in international auctions and online.

Types of Grimoires

Spell Books: A book of spells with instructions, ingredients, and illustrations for spells written or found.

Journals: Invaluable for budding witches. A catchall book containing chronicles of your beliefs, journey as a witch, progress achieved, the stumbling blocks, and personal thoughts. These are written in unstructured formats.

Pocket Grimoire: A portable notebook containing emergency and basic spells, herbs, ingredients, crystals, and ideas that strike you along the way.

Dream Book: Similar in style to the journal, it's a chronological record of dreams, astral travels, dream interpretation, symbolism, and out of body projections.

Subject-Specific Grimoire: These come in different sizes, styles, and subject categories according to the witchcraft style practiced or studied. You can have grimoires for tarot, runes, and sigils, herbology, or astrology.

Religious Grimoire: This is used in documenting your religious beliefs. It may also contain devotional practices, prayers, and holy days.

Montage Grimoire: A general-purpose grimoire. This manuscript represents your entire practice. It is when you find it challenging to organize your craft into categories.

Questions to Ask Yourself Before Starting a Grimoire/Book of Shadows

1. Does size matter to you? Do you prefer a handy text or one you only whip out on special occasions?

2. Do you intend to make daily entries? Would you rather write in it on special occasions like when casting, on sabbat, or during full or new moons?

3. What would your entries look like? Do you want an instructional grimoire? Would you want to include your musings, art, or dreams?

4. What role do you envision your book playing? Is it a guide or a confidant? What are your intentions toward it?

5. Would you want a private manuscript, or would you prefer the one you could write into together with a partner or other coven members?

6. Where would you keep your book? How about on your altar, a safe deposit box, an indoor safe, or perhaps a hole in the floorboards?

7. Would you make the book yourself, purchase one, or go digital?

8. What are the wishes for your book in the event of your demise? Do you want it passed down, entrusted to another, or destroyed?

The answers to these questions will help you in crafting, storing, and determining the flow of your book. No two grimoires or Books of Shadows can be the same, even if twins wrote them. To really make it yours you could embed pictures, zodiac signs, images of deities, botanicals, your spirit animal, tarot cards, or the eye of Horus, anything is fine. It's *your* book.

Inclusion Criteria

There is no hard and fast rule for what the contents of your book should be. There are, however, universal inclusions.

Traditions or Laws of the Coven: Principles vary from group to group; thus, it is advised to note such practices at the beginning of your book. If you are an eclectic witch or part of a tradition with no set rules, you could write down suitable rules for practicing magic. Great examples are the Three-fold law and the Wiccan Rede.

Dedication: If you are part of a coven, you could write a detailed experience of your initiation ceremony. Self-dedications to deities could be penned down, too, along with why the God was chosen. Your write-up could be a sentence or a lengthy essay. An example could be "I (name) dedicate myself to the service of the Triple Goddess, today, February 20, 2020."

Chosen Deities: This depends on what pantheon you choose. You could be monotheistic (one God) or polytheistic (many Gods). If you have a collection of different spiritual paths or myths concerning a deity you love, keep track of celestial influence by writing them down.

Correspondence Tables: All spell casters agree that correspondence tables are vital tools. They contain crystal and herb images, lunar phases, and their uses. For an entire year, tables can be plotted using a Wiccan almanac, with lunar phases, corresponding dates, and research on herbs suitable for ingestion.

The Wheel of the Year: This contains eight holidays for witches. Include this, along with sabbats, esbats, rituals, and rites for honoring your ancestors. You can decide to have a fixed routine or change things up with every festivity. Include notes on casting circles; house, healing, or prosperity blessings; and drawing down the moon to celebrate the mother Goddess.

Divination: This contains forms of divination like astrology, scrying, crystal gazing, or palmistry. Record all you learn and your experiences divining for yourself and others.

Magical Texts: Apart from the Pagan and Wiccan texts you have in your library, include information from manuscripts that appeal to you, such as *To Ride a Silver Broomstick* or *The Spiral Dance.* Old invocations and prayers in ancient languages are welcome too.

Kitchen Witchery: Many witches are always brewing one thing or the other in their kitchen. As you develop recipes for spells, food recipes for sabbat, oils, or herbal blends, keep them in your book. Apart from having them handy when you need them, it would be a fun gift to pass down to members of your lineage that might be interested in witchcraft.

Spell Work: This is optional. You may choose to write your spells in a separate book (grimoire) or your Book of Shadows. If you keep your spells and other topics in a single book, it is better to organize them, especially if they are original. Remember to leave room for documenting the time of casting, outcome, partners in casting (if any), and adjustments.

Keeping a Grimoire

The Book of Shadows is a book containing magical practices, rituals, traditions, and whatever you wish to document about your magic. Wiccan purists advocate for handwritten ones, but the advent of technology in the 21st century has made that idea obsolete. There is no single way to make this book, so use what works best for you. This is a sacred text that should be blessed along with your magical tools. If the contents are handwritten, make sure they are written legibly. This way, it is easier to read or memorize rituals.

Organizing Your Book of Shadows (BOS)

You can make your BOS yourself or buy one from the store or website. Three-ringed binders are best to allow written recipes to be entered or tweaked as needed. With this style, you could invest in sheet protectors to prevent ritual drippings, candle wax, and ink from bleeding onto and staining the page.

Include your craft name in standard letters or secret scripts with the book title at the front of the page. Spells must be legibly written. Whether you choose to write in plain English or some other lettering, be sure it's easy for you to read.

The greatest challenge is keeping it organized. You can use various materials such as a table of contents at the beginning or a detailed index at the back. Continuous study will guide you on which information to include and what to get rid of. Note the details of magical books you have read and information sources. This way, it's easier if you have to share information with others. Ringed binders make information inclusion and exclusion easier.

Many witches keep separate books, one for original creations and the other for information downloaded off the Internet. Digital grimoires should be kept encrypted and stored on flash drives, compact disks, or in the cloud for easy virtual access. One on a hard disk is no less valid than that copied by hand onto parchment.

Organization Tips for Your Book

Begin your grimoire with a blessing, poem, or inspirational quote: it's always more meaningful when it's something you crafted yourself. Ask the Goddess for protection and guidance. Write with intention, because each entry into your book is a magic ritual in itself. You could use a different poem, blessing, or saying for every entry or the same one for all.

Spell Sorting: Have separate pages or columns for everyday spells and special occasion spells. For instance, ritual baths, protection, and healing spells could be in the regular category, during sabbats and handfasting rituals in the special occasion category.

Arrange by Topic: If arranging by category proves to be a hassle, you could have a table of contents to classify spells by topic or purpose. Sections for protection could have black indexes, love sections may have pink indexes, and abundance sections could be green.

Organize by Component: This form of arrangement sorts spells according to their ingredients. Organize your book by having separate sections for candle magic, herbal poultices, crystal magic, and so on. Sorting this way tells you at a glance what spells to perform using ingredients you have at hand.

Date Each Entry: This may seem unnecessary, but without dates, how can you tell the time that elapsed between when a spell was cast and when it manifested? Apart from this, dated entries place your thoughts and experiences in a context that helps you take account of your spiritual journey over time.

Record Spell Work: After casting a spell, note it down. Include relevant information like the reason for the spell, if it was personal or cast on behalf of another, where it was cast, if anyone participated, magical tools used, and steps taken.

The Digital BOS

If you are tech-savvy and prefer your BOS on the go, you might want to consider a digital one. There are various apps you can use, should you choose this route. A phone, tablet, or laptop would suffice for an accessible and editable Book of Shadows. Even better, it fits in your pocket, purse, or suitcase. Google Keep Notes, Microsoft OneNote, or DraftPad help in creating simple files and folders.

Need a digital magic journal? Try apps like SomNote, Diaro, and Journey. The Gilded digital Book of Shadows is an all-in-one app with 40+ digital stickers, spell work templates, and four cover page options, among other features.

Encrypt and upload notes for your grimoire using ByWord, SimpleNote, and iAWriter to store, access, and print files seamlessly over various devices. When upgrading to new software, convert files to the new format to allow easy access and don't forget, create back-ups of everything!

Crafting Your Grimoire

Early grimoires were written on papyrus, parchment, or paper. Bindings were made of ornately carved wood, velvet or another tapestry, richly tooled leather or engraved metal, depending on the materials the author was able to procure. Wealthy witches and occultists decorated theirs with gold leaf accents and gemstones.

Witches of modest means decorated theirs with dried flowers and inscribed magic on stone or pieces of tree bark. If you are a witch that's "going green," then consider recycling old paper to make your own. There is a lot of information on the Internet for that purpose. The website https://www.paperslurry.com/ teaches how to make new paper from old pieces.

If your book cover is made of cloth, sew cute pockets into it to store herbs, gems, and other small magical objects. Soft covers can have holes drilled into them so that bindings are formed using natural materials like twine, vines, or ribbons. Use only high-quality paper so that your ink does not bleed. You must-have grimoire pages that lie flat and don't move around and disturb the momentum of your spell work. If your book is large, invest in a bookstand so the book does not crowd your altar.

The Difference Between a BOS and a Grimoire

Most Wiccans keep a BOS but not a grimoire, some keep both, and a few keep neither as a matter of personal taste. So, the question is, "What's the difference between these two?" Think of a BOS as a witch's diary. It has records of experiences, rituals, discussions with otherworldly entities, discoveries on the path of the Goddess, dreams, and other information of importance and preference. It is where you express your creativity without criticism or censorship. It could also contain spell work and random magical workings to monitor your progress spiritually. This way, you can see what works and what doesn't.

A grimoire is similar to a BOS, but the former is not as personal. Grimoires are a witch's textbook or manual. If you had a journal and a manual or textbook, you could tell which one would stay on the bedside table and which one should go on the shelf. A grimoire contains spells, rites, potions, and how to prepare, handle, and treat magical tools. It also has a detailed table of correspondence, magic tables, lunar phases, crystals, herbs, food recipes, colors, and research. It has no personal musings or records of spells cast, with whom, why, and where. As a beginner witch, you could decide to use one notebook as both a magical diary and an encyclopedia for rituals and spells.

As your spirit, beliefs, and craft evolve, you could take some time to organize them into two separate books. This way, you can share your research with others without exposing your private thoughts. Both books should be consecrated and handled with care. A grimoire can be kept on your altar, in a shelf or drawer for easy access, while a book of shadows should be kept somewhere safe and away from prying eyes since it is very personal.

If you have both books in one, then squirrel it away to a private hidey-hole of your choosing. If you choose to show your BOS to anyone, it must be someone you trust who will not cause harm to you or the book by disclosing its contents, treating it carelessly, or making markings on it without your permission.

Lastly, every grimoire is a Book of Shadows, but not every Book of Shadows is a grimoire. I believe that what goes into your BOS or grimoire should be as unique as you are. Purists insist that grimoires should be functional, instructional, bleeding with annotations, information, and practical application. They argue that thoughts have no place in such a manuscript. But as a witch, you must agree that it is difficult, if not impossible, to separate your feelings or thoughts from your craft. They are all part of your identity. After all, you are human, and not a cupboard.

BOS/Grimoire Security

The Book of Shadows or grimoire may be your creation, but some ethical challenges exist. Take note of this, especially if you are new to witchcraft.

1. In keeping with the Wiccan tradition of secrecy, do not list the real names, phone numbers, house addresses, or emails of fellow Wiccans or coveners. Your book may contain initials, pseudonyms, or craft names, but ensure they cannot be traced to valid names or contact information.

2. Be careful about sharing your book with cowans. Even if you are out and proud, you don't want to violate the confidences of other casters listed in your book. Extra caution should be exercised in digital or online variants of your BOS.

3. Don't touch another witch's book without permission. Many witches feel these texts are imbued with a personal power that may be diminished or disturbed when in contact with another's energy.

4. If your book includes spells or rituals that are unoriginal, don't forget to list the caster's or author's craft name. Otherwise, state that the creation isn't yours.

5. If you are oathbound concerning some information, note such vows in your book. Otherwise, you may forget later.

6. List instructions on how your book should be handled upon your demise. Many covens and ancient traditions require they be destroyed or entrusted to fellow coveners in such circumstances. Whether you are solitary or belong to a coven, protect your legacy by ensuring someone trustworthy takes care of it.

7. Put a protection spell on your BOS for security reasons. The grove and grotto, pentacle, and Celtic knot are great examples of Wiccan protective emblems. If you are super protective, place a lock on the cover of your book or buy one fashioned that way. Invest in a drawstring pouch or silk wrap to protect it from ambient energies and dust mites.

8. You could choose to make all or some entries in your book using code, so the information contained stays secret. This way, if someone else stumbles upon the contents, they won't translate them easily. You could try some ancient scripts including Theban, Pictish, Ogam Bethluisnion, Egyptian hieroglyphics, Germanic/Danish/Swedish or Norse/Scandinavian/Seax Wiccan runes, Malachim, Angelic, or Passing the river.

The Witches Alphabet: Theban Script

A	H	O	V
B	I	P	W
C	J	Q	X
D	K	R	Y
E	L	S	Z
F	M	T	
G	N	U	

ANCIENT EGYPT
HIEROGLYPHICS

A	B	C	D	E	F	G
H	I	J	K	L	M	N
O	P	Q	R	S	T	U
V	W	X	Y	Z		

Chapter Seven: Unlocking Divination and Psychic Powers

It's surprising how divination has endured through time, especially with the Catholic Church's vision for the world in the Middle Ages. There wasn't much in the way of entertainment, so divination and other forms of "heresy" were punishable by public humiliation and beheading (at best) or being boiled alive.

It's amusing to cynics and religious scholars because the Church in parts of Britain and Europe during these times practiced Bibliomancy, a form of divination using the Bible. Some followers believed that opening it at random provided answers to questions and revealed fortunes. Children with insomnia had the Bible (a religious grimoire, if we're honest) placed on their heads. Pregnant women were read verses to assure safe delivery. Anyone accused of witchcraft was weighed against the Bible and, if found wanting, they were killed. But I digress. This chapter isn't about the battle of grimoires.

Divination is rooted in the late Middle English word "divinare," meaning, "to predict." It's the opportunity given to you to gain knowledge, to tap into our collective subconscious mind. This raises your awareness to see past, present, and future events. Many witches practice some form of divination, which gives indispensable spiritual and psychological advice when they need to make critical decisions in life.

Man has not begun to scratch the surface as to how many methods of divination exist. In ancient Babylon, Priests divined using haruspic, which sounds like a dish but is actually divination using animal entrails or oil drops in a water basin. This chapter aims to discuss the popular divination forms that exist and some misconceptions about them.

Choosing a System

There are hundreds of systems available, each with books dedicated to their study. The choice is entirely up to you. If you wish to add divination to your spiritual practice, I suggest you don't spend a fortune on it until you are sure it appeals to you. Don't be a system junkie.

Test systems available to you. If you're using tarot, for instance, ask the same question in different ways to check the consistency of your answers. Note them down in your BOS so you can keep records of their effectiveness. Choose a form of divination that speaks to you, provides you with clear messages, and isn't difficult for you to master.

Understand that results or answers from any method do not mean your fate (or that of another) is sealed. The future isn't set in stone. Check out styles and systems from your history and culture. I recommend this because you are probably already familiar with its symbolism. If a deity from a specific culture, like the Mayan It-Zamn or Celtic Morrigan, fascinates you, you may choose a system from such origins.

Popular Forms of Divination

Pendulum Dowsing: Ancient Greeks and Romans used this to predict the future. It's the simplest form of divination to learn because it answers only with a yes, no, or maybe. This method can be used to find lost pets or objects, identify allergies, figure out your purpose, detect negative energies, find ley lines or water, and so much more. It works by receiving and transmitting energy using intuition, decoding messages from guardian angels and other spiritual masters. A variety of pendulums are available. There's no need to buy an expensive one to get good results. Some people use something as simple as a key suspended on a string.

Make yours using a stone or crystal wrapped with jewelers' wire and a lightweight chain of about ten to fourteen inches, or invest in one made of clear quartz, a gem that promotes clarity of mind and connection to a higher purpose. Amethyst and rose quartz are also good options. You can have more than one pendulum. Always remember to cleanse and charge them after use. Wrap in silk or keep in drawstring pouches for safety.

Tasseomancy: This comes from the French word "tasse," meaning cup, and the Greek "mancy," meaning "to divine." Tasseomancy involves interpreting patterns in tealeaves, wine sediments, or coffee grounds. It has origins in Asia, the Middle East, and Ancient Greece.

Chinese in the 2nd millennium B.C.E. started divining using loose tealeaves, which left patterns at the bottom of a cup. Modern tasseography developed in the 17th century after trade routes brought tea to Europe from China. As tea consumption spread throughout Europe, so did tasseomancy. Crescent moons signify fame, elephants mean good health, birds bring good luck, and triangles good fortune.

Numerology: This is divination using numbers. It's founded on the basis that each number has a unique energy signature that gives insight into one's character and destiny in life. Some numbers hold more power compared to others. The three primary forms of this system are Qabbalic, Chaldean, and Pythagorean. One or a combination of two or all three can be used in a reading, but it's safer to use one consistently to avoid confusing results.

Kabbalistic numerology is derived from Jewish mysticism. The Hebrew alphabet and its twenty-two vibrations are used in name interpretation. Chaldean numerology began in Mesopotamia, the home of Western astrology. It is closely linked to planetary associations. In this system, single digits show your outer nature, while double digits your inner qualities.

Pythagoras developed Pythagorean numerology in the sixth century, and he used it to predict individual destinies and the fate of places. He went a step further to alter people's future by changing their names.

In modern numerology, your life path is the sum of the numbers in your birth date reduced to a single digit from one to nine. The exception is when they add up to master numbers like eleven, twenty-two, and thirty-three. The destiny number is the sum of your name as it appears on your birth certificate. The sum of consonants in your name reveals your personality number, and the vowels sum up your soul number.

Rune Casting: The runic alphabet (Futhark) is a writing system developed by the Germanic dwellers of Scandinavia, Iceland, Northern Europe, and Britain in the third century. Legend states Futhark was discovered by Odin while hanging upside down from the branches of Yggdrasil for nine days. Futhark has twenty-four letters.

Rune is a Proto-Germanic word meaning "mystery" or "secret." In Finnish, it means "poem," and in Lithuanian, "to speak." In old English, the word "ridan" meant, "interpreting runes," while "writan" meant, "carving runes." It's possible these were the same words adapted in modern English as "read" and "write." Runic letters have been found on jewelry and weapons dating back to the third century. Futhark is more than just letters. It represents the cosmic forces of the universe and the Gods themselves.

Rune casting is a method that uses runes laid out in a specific pattern or randomly to guide you in problem solving and decision-making. Think of it like magic scrabble. There's no general method for casting, but standard layouts include the three-rune cast and nine-rune cast. Runes are made of different materials, whether bone, crystals, clay, wood, or metal. You can purchase them or create your own.

The theory behind rune casting is that it focuses on the conscious and subconscious minds at once. Don't expect specific answers like when you will marry, die, or become a millionaire. Don't expect concrete advice either. Runes only offer suggestions or possible outcomes based on the present state of affairs. Answers given are not random. Your subconscious provides them. Use runes when you need clarity on an issue or only see the incomplete picture.

I Ching or Yi Jing or Book of Changes: This is an ancient Chinese oracular text used in cleromancy (casting lots). This system started in China to provide answers to life's questions. Early methods involved tossing fifty yarrow sticks, but with time, coins were used. I Ching uses six random numbers between six and nine, arranged in the King Wen sequence—a hexagram of six lines, formed by reeds or coins.

Hexagram lines provide predictions about the past and near future. This form of divination is based on the theory of the five elements:

- Huo (fire).
- Jin (metal).
- Shui (water).
- Tu (Earth).
- Mu (wood).

These elements form the basis of all that exists in the universe. I Ching is also founded on the concept of Yin and Yang, which is the concept of dualism and the interconnectedness of all things, as well as Bagua, the cosmic permutations showing the fundamental principles of reality represented in eight trigrams and sixty-four hexagrams.

In this style of divination, three coins are tossed six times (for hexagram lines). Patterns are formed when they land, and they determine answers to specific problems. I Ching is unique because it does not provide you with clear explanations. It only helps you tap into the solutions lying within you. No matter the toss, what matters is your mindset because the focus is needed to interpret the answers from your subconscious.

Palmistry or Chiromancy: Studying the hands is how this form of divination is accomplished. The palmist examines the lines on your palm together with your hand shape and size in relation to finger length. You can learn a lot about a person's mental, physical, and emotional makeup from their hands. Details about their past, present, and future can also be revealed.

Palmistry has been practiced for over 3000 years, becoming popular in the Zhou dynasty. Different forms of this science exist in many cultures worldwide, but the most prominent include the methods taught in Vedic astrology, Romani culture, and Chinese practices.

The left-hand reveals innate characteristics and makes up 20% of the reading, while the right-hand shows post-natal information comprising 80% of readings. Since your hands are continuously changing, information divined from two years ago may differ slightly from a more recent reading. These are the major lines that matter and what they represent:

- Heart line: Passion, love, and intimacy.
- Head line: Wisdom and intelligence.
- Life line: Vitality, patterns of illness that may arise.
- Fate line: Career, destiny.

From its inception, palmistry has always been a revered psychic science. Great leaders like Alexander the Great selected soldiers for his commanding troops based on their palm readings. Islam, Christianity, and scientists have dismissed this as "hocus-pocus." No matter how you want to slice it, the hand is a masterpiece. Even science agrees. That's why there is a whole field of study for fingerprints and the hand called dactylography. Dusting for prints is the staple in every crime scene. What more proof do you need to believe your hands hold power?

Scrying: Scrying comes from an old English word, "descry," meaning, "to make out dimly." Here, you gaze into a reflective, refractive, translucent, or luminescent surface to see images that reveal events. Surfaces include crystal balls, water, clouds, polished obsidian, mirrors, or candle flames, polished gemstones, fishing hooks, eggs, and polished metals. Some prefer staring at the insides of their eyes, which is called eyelid scrying.

Scrying is not only associated with gypsies. Different cultures use it. Egyptians used ink on water. The Egyptian Goddess Hathor had a shield that reflected all things in their true form. It's from this shield the first magic mirror was designed. Ancient Persian texts written in the tenth century mentioned the Cup of Jamshid used by occultists to observe all seven layers of the universe.

Ancient Celts, Aztecs, and Greeks scried using black glass, beryl, crystal, polished quartz, and water. Nostradamus, for instance, divined using a bowl of water on a brass tripod. Mesopotamians used bowls of oil. Ancient Arabs used polished thumbnails. John Dee, personal magician to Queen Elizabeth I, used polished obsidian and a small crystal egg presently kept in the British Museum, London.

It's believed mirrors and other shiny surfaces are doorways to the spirit world, allowing messages and warnings from loved ones and other entities to be delivered through its highly reflective surface. Witches and shamans often covered their scrying mediums in black fabric when not in use to keep these "doorways" closed.

Tarot: This is a form of cartomancy—predicting the future, understanding the present, and gaining insight into the past using cards. Tarot decks have seventy-eight cards with four suits containing fourteen cards each (ten number cards and four court cards) called the minor arcana, and twenty-two trump cards, called the major arcana. Arcana is Latin for "mysteries" or "secrets." Tarots help in self-understanding, insight, prediction, guidance, and healing.

No one knows the true origin of tarot. Occultists and tarot experts like Eliphas Lévi and Etteilla suggest they originated from ancient Egypt. Others claim it's a Chinese invention. There is no sufficient evidence to support either theory. The story that seems more likely is the Romani brought tarot into Europe. Although the exact date is unknown, such cards have existed as early as the fourteenth century.

Each picture on the tarot has a symbolic meaning. The major arcana represents life-changing decisions, beginning with the fool (0) and ending with the world (XXI). They indicate your journey physically and spiritually through life, after which you die and become reborn to start at zero. The minor arcana comprises swords, cups, pentacles, and wands. Court cards include the king, queen, and page (or princess in some decks).

They represent your personality type, individual understanding of situations, and other people. Numbered cards show the different stages of an event, starting with the ace card and ending with ten. Each card has an upright and a reversed interpretation. You could read both sides or turn it upright.

The classic deck is the Rider-Waite deck, which is the choice for beginners and experts alike. Some believe your first deck should be gifted to you. This is a popular misconception since you can't pick and choose with gifts. It's more rewarding to pick a deck that speaks to you. Do you prefer the classics or modern ones? No deck is better than another, so take stock of your emotions as you browse on or offline.

Divination Spells

Temperance Scrying Spell

You'll need a still body of water, or water in a chalice, as well as a Temperance card.

First, look at the Temperance or Angel card (XIV). It will put you in the right frame of mind for scrying. Focus on it with an open mind, trusting that you will receive the right information. Let it imbue you with its energy.

Chant:

"Temperance card and water still,

increase my vision, grant my will.

Reveal the truth, so knowledge is gained,

and images dance past the reflective plane."

Meditation: Focus on your reflective surface, which is the water. Feel the exchange of energy from the card to the water. You may imagine this as white light moving back and forth between the card and the water. Doing this sharpens your ability to scry and raises your endurance levels. Project the card above the scrying surface in your mind's eye and feel its energy flow through you. Thank the angel for its guidance while keeping your eyes on your reflective surface. Let the energy flow unhindered between the water and you. Remain that way until you have a vision.

Right Decision Spell

For this spell, you will need the Two of Pentacles and the Hanged Man cards.

This spell is one of guidance, especially if you are in a pickle. Ensure it's performed at least twenty-four hours before your final decision. The Two of Pentacles symbolizes the balance between choices, while the Hanged Man represents one stuck in a web of indecision.

First, place the Hanged Man before you. He is the symbol of the crossroads. Free yourself from the Hang Man's clutches, as the failure to make a decision is a decision also.

Next, place the Two of Pentacles before you. Consider the choices you have.

Chant:

"Resolutions, resolutions, choices are they all.

Reveal to me the bigger picture; never will I fall.

Safely protected, free I will be.

Pick the option best suited to me."

Juggle the decisions you have to make in your mind until one hits you as the right choice. Deliberate on the pros and cons of your choice for twenty-four hours before officially announcing it.

Chapter Eight: The Power of Invocation

Since the dawn of time, humans have been curious and sensitive to the otherworldly realm. Invisible to the human eye, it affects us daily. Our ancestors held knowledge of these worlds and carved animals and other instruments to represent and control them.

The spirit worlds, the astral, planetary, elemental, and celestial all have entities passively interacting with you in the physical plane. Your aim as an occultist, witch, or Wiccan is to stay sensitive to these worlds, intuitively sense their messages, and actively communicate with the beings in such worlds. One of the steps taken to communicate with otherworldly entities actively is an invocation.

What Invocation Is

Invocation is the practice of inviting a deity, spirit, or entity's presence to use their powers or for their ability to grant a desire. They are a form of conjuration. Invocation uses the mystical properties of sacred words, sound, and names to create alignment and harmony with these entities' consciousnesses. Invocations are composed with extreme care because they can quickly go wrong. To attract the attention of a specific spirit or force, the requester must acknowledge their attributes, strengths, and virtue, so total reverence is offered.

Invocations have one essential recommendation: they must be spoken aloud and not thought of in silence. All faculties and senses must be involved in an invocation. As many intense vibrations as possible must also accompany them because to perform invocations is to incense oneself with prayer.

During magic, invocations are done while casting a sacred circle to implore the presence of specific spirits to witness and offer protection during a ritual. It is also done to allow for temporary possession, as seen in mediumship, trance rituals, and channeling. The most sought after uses of invocation include:

- Healing.
- Wealth generation.
- Finding love.
- Protection against the evil eye, enemies, and bad luck.
- Increasing chances of conception.

Grimoires and other magical manuals contain numerous ritualistic instructions and invocations. Orthodox Christianity also has rites involving the invocation of their deity, in this case, God. The Lord's Prayer, for instance, is a popular invocation. Pagans and occultists invoke deities as well. The only difference is that rites are not limited to a single God but other Gods of different pantheons according to the purposes these deities are best suited for.

Another difference between Christian invocations and those done by practitioners of the occult is that the occultists go one step further than benedictions and the Eucharist. They either become one with the invoked deity, or manipulate the influence of the forces invoked, affixing such powers to a consecrated weapon, amulet, or talisman.

Purposes of Invocation

1. To become one with the deity, speak and act as it would, and serve as an oracle. This happens in African voodoo, although invocation is showcased via ritualistic ecstatic dancing.

2. To confer blessings on an individual or bestow on them a measure of power. For instance, the laying of hands during initiation bestows power.

3. To command as the entity would, the spirits under his control to come to the invoker's aid. For example, invoking Lucifuge Rofocale may cause demons under his command like Marbas, Bael, and Agares to be evoked. If you invoke Thoth, the Egyptian God of wisdom, writing, and the moon, you might provoke an effective evocation of Hermes, the Greek form of Thoth, or Mercury, Thoth's Roman counterpart.

4. To enable the practitioner to capture the essence and virtue of the deity, so this energy can be used to charge an amulet or talisman, which stays efficacious long after the ritual ceases.

5. To manipulate the energy of a deity or force in the same way as one would the elements in order to charge elemental weapons.

Example of an Invocation Calling the Four Quarters in a Ritual

"I summon the lord and lady fair,

I call unto me the element of air

I implore the ancients with wisdom of old,

To stay present this night, my spirit to hold.

Lord and lady safeguard me, keep me far from harm

May the element of air entrust me with charm.

Oh, ancient ones, favor me with knowledge that lasts

Provide for me within the circle cast.

I entreat the lord and lady to hear my plea

I call to me the element of water

I invoke the ancients bearing truth from beyond

Be present this night, as sure as it's long.

Lord and lady, keep me safe, close to your side

Let the element of water fill me with feelings of pride,

May the old ones grant to me patience that lasts

And stay present on this night in the circle cast.

I summon the lord and lady that gave me birth,

I call upon the element of earth

To shine upon me their divine light.

Lord and lady protect and overshadow me with love.

So, the earth empowers me below and above

May the old ones grant me the wisdom that lasts,

Provide for me in this circle cast.

I summon you with whole desire

And call to me the element of fire

I beseech the old ones, forever ancient and wise

To bring me comfort, silence yearnings, and heed my cries.

Protect me, lord and lady, with your power to heal

May fire protect me beyond the strength of steel

May the old ones grant me insight that lasts

And grant me provision in the circle cast."

Feel free to use this ritual or make one of your own using this as a template.

The Concept of Evocation

Evocation is a spiritual practice where you call out to or call forth a spirit (benign or malignant) to take form outside your body in the form of energy. It's the practice used to get in touch with ancestors or familiars for the very first time. Evocative rituals are done to understand these spirits' true nature and get to know them before allowing them in your life. These entities and familiars become close to us in time, but only after a relationship is established.

In evocation, there is no direct line of communication with the entity summoned. It never comes in contact with your physical form, although you can see and perceive its presence. They can't possess us, manipulate us, or take charge of our vital force because they lack our express permission. Some magical traditions perform evocation ceremonies by employing the use of mind-altering substances with or without utterances.

Manuals such as the *Lemegeton, Claviculis Salomonis,* and the *Sacred Magic of Abra-Melin the Mage* provide detailed instructions and devotions dedicated to the summoning of one or a cadre of entities, deceased relatives, and other familiar spirits.

In these manuals, entities were commanded using long Hellenic and Kabbalistic litanies in the name of God. The summoner also used staves, wands, fire, incense, complex diagrams drawn on parchment or other surfaces, and daggers.

Enochian magic allowed evocation via a mirror or crystal ball. The seer or volunteer becomes attuned to the entity's voice and can pass on required messages to the evoker. Sometimes, the volunteer is a medium, speaking as the entity, not on its behalf. In some cases, the entity may be contained in a symbolic artifact or conjured into a shape or diagram from which it cannot escape without the conjurer's express permission.

In occult practices, evocations may involve summoning a demon, sublunary, or an unpredictable entity. In the *Salomonis Regis* or *Lesser Key of King Solomon*, there are explicit instructions for the practitioner to perform demonic evocations. This is done with a magical triangle drawn to contain the evoked entity and a magically sealed circle for the summoner's protection.

The problem with this is that repeated performance of this ritual over extended periods puts you at the risk of embodying the traits of the entity you are subconsciously evoking. This is similar to how we copy the actions of friends we associate with the most. When this happens in a spiritual connotation, it is the summoner or occultist's responsibility to remain aware of such subconscious influences. It is they who must draw the proverbial line, which they should never cross unless they are willing to soak up the attributes of this spirit permanently. This is why occult practitioners must possess more control of their subconscious compared to the average person.

The Difference Between Invocation and Evocation

To invoke an entity is to call it into your being. This allows you to assume some or all of its characteristics or essence. You become one with the entity you call upon. Invoking is a very intimate act, and its results entail a far more intense level of potential and communication.

Invocations require the summoner to become something of a medium. The entity summoned is meant to come from within them. When you invoke, you use all your energies and resources to ensure it happens. After a successful invocation, the spirit acts through the summoner. Several changes might occur from vocal alteration to physical demeanor and appearance. Many who have been in such positions claim to be aware of the entity using them as a vessel. Others experience severe dissociation and time gaps.

Evocation differs in that the summoner is conjuring an entity for a particular favor, information, or some task aimed at practical manifestation in the physical plane. After completing the task, the practitioner may choose to banish, bind, or dismiss the entity. There isn't servitude or supplication to the entity. The aim is for the entity to grant favors or answer questions. The practitioner may decide to give an offering to the entity as courtesy demands. Vital to evocation is this distance created by the practitioner between the entity and the summoner.

To Invoke, Evoke, or Do Both?

There are many methods of evoking and invoking spirits. The most common forms are visualization, Ouija boards, automatic writing, pendulums, and dreams. The choice to invoke or evoke is dependent on the entity in question and its nature. Even with fellow humans, there are different degrees of interaction, all dependent on your degree of closeness with the person. You wouldn't go and hug a total stranger in the alley, would you?

When evoking or invoking any entity, like Mammon, for instance, would you want to summon him because you are obsessed with money without learning the full implication of working with him? Never forget, single-focused obsession is unhealthy and can cloud your judgment, blinding you to the price of certain actions. What if, after becoming filthy rich, you discover money no longer holds the appeal and value it once had? What then? You become enslaved by the demon you summoned.

So, when diving headfirst into invoking or embodying a particular spirit, consider all options. You can't go about summoning entities simply because you possess the knowledge or feel it's an excellent idea for the summer break because that "cool" idea can quickly go awry. These are matters of serious thought. Before attempting to evoke or invoke, verify that the entity's attributes are in alignment with your needs. Your end goals must come first. Don't put your cart before the horse. The Wiccan Rede may allow you to do what you will but be prepared for consequences.

Apart from your goals, it's crucial to consider your abilities. You've heard the popular saying, "Where attention goes, energy flows." Working with magical forces and spiritual energies can be thrilling, rewarding, and altogether powerful, but caution must be practiced. Proper education on magical rituals and powers is necessary, along with a receptive mindset. A lack of these two can place you in a situation where you are faced with energies you haven't the slightest idea how to manage.

Budding occultists wonder if one can evoke and invoke at the same time. It's possible. The question is, is it necessary? For instance, you wish to invoke and evoke Orobas, the Goetic entity. To summon him is to embody his wisdom and ability to win the hearts of friends and foes alike. You evoke him to remain faithful to you, reveal answers to the past, present, and future, and protect you from harm and the temptation of other entities. To be candid, it's brewing a storm in a teacup.

Invocation already contains the effects of evocation to a degree. The impact on the physical plane is observed in both cases, the difference is only that evocation stops you from embodying the entity you've called forth. Now, what if you decide to invoke one spirit and evoke another.

Let's invoke Orobas once again and evoke another entity, say Astaroth. Both are powerful entities, but their capabilities nullify each other. The former forces you to embody honesty, while the latter has rationalized his personal philosophies that may or may not tally with the truth.

The only condition under which it's okay to summon two entities at a time is if their attributes complement each other in fulfilling your goals. So, instead of Astaroth, you evoke Andromalius. His characteristics of punishing evildoers and dishonest dealers complement Orobas's honesty.

Whatever you do, don't go summoning more than a single entity as a beginner. There is a lot of training required to effectively summon, command, bind, and banish an entity. Additional training and experience are needed to coax certain entities into yielding more power or offering more favors than they usually would. Inexperience or distractions during invocations/evocations will make you powerful spiritual enemies, leaving you bound in a pact that you never bargained for or imagined. On this note, do not split your focus and resources between many tasks and entities simultaneously.

Chapter Nine: Crystal Magic and Alchemy

For ages, crystals, regardless of their size, have been regarded as a gift of the Gods to man. Like humans, these stones have unique vibrational energies. You can use them on their own or enhance your magic. Many crystals exist, most of them with overlapping uses and properties. You can purchase them online, in New Age shops, or at spirit fairs. You may also receive them as a gift, stumble upon them in a quarry, riverbed, or a hike through the woods. In this chapter, we'll go over some versatile stones, their medicinal properties, and metaphysical significance.

Forms of Crystal Energy

Projective Crystals: These are similar to the Yang energy. They project energy, are masculine in nature, and associated with air and fire elements as seen in their vibrant colors, sounds, and energies. They tend to have colors linked to blood or sunlight with red, gold, orange, and yellow hues. They are ideal for healing and protection from evil energy. They are necessary stones to have when in need of a boost in willpower, vitality, self-esteem, strength, and determination.

Examples include tiger's eye, bloodstone, ruby, carnelian, citrine, red jasper, amber, cinnabar, onyx, et cetera.

Receptive Crystals: These are associated with Yin energy. They absorb energy and are feminine in nature, related to the elements of water and earth. These stones always impart a feeling of serenity, spiritual grounding, and the promotion of psychic abilities. Their hues are in the cooler aspect of the color spectrum like purple, blue, silver, white, green, brown, grey, and pink. They are ideal for increasing love, peace, compassion, psychic abilities, and healing the subconscious mind. In this category, popular crystals include turquoise, moonstone, malachite, lapis lazuli, jade, rose quartz, aqua aura, labradorite, chrysocolla, et cetera.

Some crystals fall into neither category. They have dual properties of projection and reception depending on their type and the energy you attune with during spell work. Clear quartz, golden healer quartz, opal, amethyst, ametrine, and many black crystals fall into the dual power category as well. As you read and practice more crystal magic, you become more aware of the energy crystals contain.

Versatile Stones Everyone Should Own

Amethyst: A variant of the quartz family, its colors range from lilac to a deep royal purple. This stone's quality is its color zoning, as areas of the gem have angular zones of darker to light colors, like the ombre effect. Its name is derived from the Greek *amethystos*, meaning "not intoxicated." This was because it was believed that this stone placed at the bottom of a drinking glass prevented its owner from drunkenness.

> **Alchemical Properties:** Amethyst water balances the hormones, cleanses the blood, relieves tension and pain, boosts the nervous system, and promotes sobriety. Sleeping with amethyst under your pillow helps in insomnia and aids you in understanding your dreams.

Mystical Properties: This stone is associated with the angel Raphael. It absorbs negativity. Its electromagnetic frequencies help in meditation, manifestation, and achieving enlightenment. Its association with the crown chakra, soma, third eye, and stellar gateway awakens your intuition and psychic abilities. It also rids you of illusions that prevent you from seeing the truth.

Black Tourmaline or Schorl: A pyroelectric and piezoelectric stone made of sodium iron aluminum borate silicate; known for its use in drawing ash from pipes in ancient times.

Alchemical Properties: It strengthens the immune system, thyroid gland, and neural pathways. It improves hand-eye coordination, aligns the spine, relieves pain, reduces inflammation, and guards against motion sickness. Tourmaline reduces the effects of electromagnetic and geomagnetic energy. It is also known to boost circulation, immunity, and metabolism as well as reduce lung problems, pain, and muscle aches.

Mystical Properties: A grounding stone, it dispels negative patterns of behavior and malevolent entities. It also confers psychic protection and is used in scrying, protection, and purification rituals.

Bloodstone: Also called heliotrope with colors ranging from deep green to dark blue-green with red or rust-colored dots, it was believed to result from blood droplets that fell from Jesus onto jasper stones at the foot of the cross.

Alchemical Properties: Powdered bloodstone mixed with egg white and honey can draw out snake venom and stop bleeding and tumor growth. (That said, please go to your doctor if you find yourself with any of these and use the bloodstone as a supplemental treatment.) It increases physical stamina, purifies the blood and kidneys, and reduces nosebleeds, acidity, and pus secretion.

Mystical Properties: It promotes psychic healing, empowers kundalini, boosts manifestation, works well with weather magic, and banishes bad vibrations.

Carnelian or Singer's Stone: Ancient Egyptians call this crystal "the setting sun" because of its rich reddish-orange or amber yellow color.

Alchemical Properties: It helps in vitamin and mineral absorption and strengthens ligaments and bones. It provides relief from rheumatism, depression, arthritis, lower back problems, increases libido, and boosts fertility. When pulverized, carnelian heals tooth and gum infections. You should see a dentist as well if you're suffering from those.

Mystical Properties: It restores courage, motivation, and creativity, provides healing from all forms of abuse, increases self-esteem, and reduces envy. It is used in talismans and amulets to prevent psychic attacks and renew lost passion.

Citrine: This is an extremely rare stone belonging to the quartz family. Its color ranges from golden yellow to orange-brown or reddish-orange.

Alchemical Properties: It is an immune strengthener and a hormone balancer. It fights degenerative diseases, chronic fatigue, and urogenital tract infections. Citrine-infused water helps the spleen and pancreas and also relieves menstrual cramps.

Mystical Properties: It rids you of toxic mindsets, attracts abundance and wealth, and also raises self-esteem and confidence. It helps overcome phobias, reduce sensitivity to criticism and anxiety, and transform negative energy into positive energy.

Clear Quartz: This is the source of the word "crystal," from the Greek word "krystallos," meaning, "clear ice." Ancient Greeks assumed the Gods who froze celestial waters formed quartz. Some say it's proof that the cities of Atlantis and Lemuria existed.

Alchemical Properties: It cleanses organs, promotes cell regeneration and tissue oxygenation. It strengthens metabolism, joints, bones, and connective tissue, heals blisters, blockages, and the body's vibrational structure.

Mystical Properties: This is an easily programmable and versatile stone. It amplifies psychic energy and vibrational fields, raises your awareness, and dispels negativity. It boosts the focus, intentions, and power of other crystals. It helps with past life recall, allows communication with animals, spirit guides, familiars, and plants. Clear quartz also increases patience, perseverance, and prosperity.

Hematite: A mineral formed from iron oxide, it comes in a variety of colors ranging from red to brown, black, and gray. Its name is derived from the Greek word "haimatites," an allusion to its rusty blood color. According to Greek myth, it was created when Saturn murdered his father, Uranus.

Alchemical Properties: It's a blood cleanser that supports the heart and nervous system and improves circulation. It rids you of addictions rooted in unfulfilled desires and emotional cravings, and it also soothes inflammation.

Mystical Properties: It improves focus and concentration, increases self-confidence and charisma, protects from physical, mental, and psychic troubles, and is an excellent grounding stone.

Jade: Highly revered by Chinese and Aztecs as a good luck charm, this is a translucent or opaque stone with colors ranging from dark green to gray, brown, yellow, white, and even black.

Alchemical Properties: It eases physical pain, accelerates healing after surgery, improves skin elasticity, prevents wrinkles, filters toxins from the blood, and supports plant growth, love, harmony, and abundance. Its muscle-relaxing properties help in respiratory problems.

Mystical Properties: It helps dream recall, banishes negativity, brings clarity and insight in toxic relationships, improves meditation and self-confidence, and purifies energy fields.

Jet: Neither crystal nor mineral, it is a mineraloid formed from fossilized driftwood, which underwent extreme pressure and decay to form a black or dark brown lightweight solid with a metallic luster similar to coal.

Alchemical Properties: It alleviates altitude sickness, viral and bacterial infections, accelerates DNA repair, and provides relief from headaches or migraines, dental pain, and stomachache.

Mystical Properties: It gives psychic protection, stabilizes and protects businesses from loss, deflects envy, helps in grounding, builds psychic powers, stimulates kundalini, protects against violence, pain, nightmares, energy vampires, and bottled feelings.

Lapis Lazuli: A symbol of cosmic correspondence, also called lazurite, this stone comes in shades of blue, from pale to indigo. It's a fusion of three minerals: pyrite, calcite, and lazurite. Valued more than gold itself, Lapis is one of the most ancient sought-after stones on Earth.

Alchemical Properties: It's an immune strengthener. It regulates the menstrual cycle, alleviates pain, reduces blood pressure, and detoxifies the body. It grants relief from attention deficit disorders, insomnia, and vertigo and heals diseases of the larynx, throat, and vocal cord.

Mystical Properties: This promotes ease of communication, inner observation, authenticity, truth, psychic protection, clarity, compassion, and wisdom. It's used in talismans to promote fidelity and friendships and increase psychic ability.

Malachite: A bright green or green crystal formed from copper carbonate.

Alchemical Properties: It clears radiation and electromagnetic pollution, helps the liver in detoxification, and treats female reproductive conditions like menstrual cramps. It treats dyslexia, vertigo, carsickness, aerophobia, epilepsy, arthritis, and diseases of the pancreas and spleen. It heals fractures, joint pains, and tumors.

Mystical Properties: Also called the transformation stone, it increases insight, dispels psychic imbalance, absorbs negative energy, and is used in prosperity spells. It also promotes empathy, discourages fear of confrontation, dissolves toxic patterns, emotional trauma, blockages, and residues from past lives. It's toxic when used in large quantities.

Moonstone or Traveler's Stone: A translucent, opalescent, pearly blue variant of the feldspar mineral orthoclase, it is found naturally in parts of India and Sri Lanka.

Alchemical Properties: It regulates the female reproductive system, supports pituitary glands, hormones, the digestive system, and reduces obesity and edema.

Mystical Properties: It increases psychic gifts and intuition. It helps you tap into your feminine energy, combats ego, stress, anger, and materialism while infusing you with very high cosmic energy. For this reason, invest in grounding stones like hematite to enable you to assimilate the moonstone's energy.

Obsidian: A silica-rich igneous rock formed from volcanic lava, black in color with a shiny luster, shamans regard it as a magic doorway through time and space. It is also called royal agate, glass agate, or volcanic glass. Snowflake, blue, apache tear, and mahogany obsidian are gentler than black variants.

Alchemical Properties: Used in making cutting and piercing tools, including some surgical scalpels, it also heals fractures, ear infections, sciatica, spinal problems, and alopecia. It strengthens the immune and lymphatic systems.

Mystical Properties: It promotes deep soul healing by exposing character flaws, clears negative constructs, increases self-assurance, self-control, strength, and awareness, and psychic protection. It also absorbs negativity from the environment and activates untapped energies. It is used for scrying, grounding, centering, and meditation, and in making athames.

Rose Quartz: Called the stone of unconditional love, it has a pale pink or rosy red color. This is due to deposits of iron, manganese, or titanium.

Alchemical Properties: It calms breathing difficulties, improves circulation, eases tension and palpitations. It alleviates eating disorders, Alzheimer's, dementia, and fatigue. It also heals burns, bruises, infertility, kidney diseases, and migraines and protects against environmental pollution.

Mystical Properties: It heals trust issues in relationships, soothes emotional pain, grief, and trauma from past and present lifetimes. It opens the heart chakra at all levels to give and receive love. It brings about peace, comfort, self-worth, and healing.

Tiger's Eye or Wolf Stone: A metamorphic rock of the chalcedony family with a silky luster, it comes in a range of colors, from reddish-brown to golden.

Alchemical Properties: It reduces blood pressure and depression, enhances night vision, assists digestion, strengthens and aligns the spine, releases toxins, repairs fractures, stabilizes mood swings, fortifies the blood, boosts fertility, and eases constrictions of the stomach and gallbladder.

Mystical Properties: It focuses the mind, promotes clarity, and reduces cravings and eating disorders. It increases dream recall, meditation abilities and awakens the kundalini. It also balances Yin-Yang energies and brain hemispheres.

You don't have to buy all these at once. Start with a few that resonate with you, then gradually add to your collection. Clean and charge your stones before and after purchase or use. When charging crystals, some experts advise charging stones with fire energy like bloodstones, carnelians, citrine, amber, and obsidian using sunlight. Stones with water energy like jade, lapis lazuli, moonstone, and jet are charged with moonlight, while earth-based stones like hematite, jasper, green jade, malachite, tiger eye, and tourmaline are charged by burying them in the earth.

Remember, these are just suggestions. Proper research must be done concerning charging, cleaning, and using crystals for mystical or medicinal purposes. Amazonite, cinnabar, emerald, malachite, pyrite, and azurite, for instance, are toxic when ingested. Kunzite, selenite, hematite, and ulexite dissolve in water. Pearl and turquoise fade with water exposure. Citrine, amethyst, aventurine, and rose quartz can fade with prolonged sun exposure. Avoid carrying wireless devices such as phones around charged stones as they interfere with their magical field.

Some Spells for Crystal Magic

House Blessing or Consecrating a Sacred Space

You will need:

- One white candle.

- One or more amethyst and quartz crystals.

- Myrrh or lemon essential oil (place a drop on each crystal).

Place the stones beside the lit candle and imagine white light radiating from it, saturating every corner of your house or space. Whisper affirmations like, "I declare this space/house a point of sacred energy. Happiness, prosperity, and wellbeing abound here. So, mote it be." After this, you may allow the candle to burn out on its own. Place the amethyst in a prominent area in your space or home, so it continues emitting positive energy.

Financial Aid Crystal Spell

You will need:

- A prosperity crystal of your choice (jade, citrine, carnelian, pyrite, moss agate).

- A note pad or piece of paper and a pen.

- One green candle.

Light the candle and write your name and specific need on the note or paper, along with the amount needed to fulfill the need. For example, "$5,000 monthly." Refrain from using words like "I need" or "I want," because this spell will amplify that energy so that you always need or want.

Fold the paper into a square, place the crystal on it, saying, "I thank the universe for its provision, with this (name of the crystal) I call forth the solution to my needs." Leave the stone on the paper until the candle burns out and bury it in a potted plant or somewhere in your compound. Don't forget where this spot is. Mark it with something if need be. Leave the stone buried until your desire is met, then dig up the crystal and paper. Offer thanks to the universe for fulfilling your desire. Showing gratitude empowers you for future spell work.

Chapter Ten: Creating Your Spells and Rituals

Experienced spell crafters are aware of magic basics and understand the flow of energy in the universe. Spell crafting teaches you how best to approach and utilize natural power, know precisely the right time to cast, how best to raise your energy, and the intricacies and ethics of fine-tuning already made spells. As your magic intensifies, you discover that personally crafted spells not only help you evolve in your craft but also strengthen your practice.

Crafting Your Spells

There are two ways of crafting spells. One is to take an already made one and make it yours to suit your individual needs. You can modify some components as long as replacements do not deviate from the intent of the spell. Deities can be replaced, specific phrases reworded to suit your heritage or spiritual beliefs. The aim is to infuse as much of your energy as you can manage, while retaining the spell's original structure.

The second method is creating an entirely new spell. Do this when you cannot find one addressing your specific needs or when already-made ones seem to have something missing. Before doing this, do research to find out appropriate correspondences and ingredients to incorporate into your spellwork. Examples of correspondences include herbs, deities, oils, incense, offerings, planets, elements, and colors. The more specific and correct your correspondences are, the more potent your spell will be.

No matter what your chosen method is, an already made or new spell, the next step to take is to draft an incantation that specifies your desire. These incantations can be poetic or have no rhyme at all. Incantations usually include invocations to a deity whose powers align with your intentions. Incantations with rhyme are traditional and seen as more potent due to inbuilt magic hidden in rhyme. As Gwen Thompson said in the 1975 issue of *Green Egg*, "To bind the spell e'ry time, let the spell be spake in rhyme."

Steps to Creating a Foolproof Spell

Step 1. Clearly Indicate Your Desire: There is no use performing a spell for the sake of it. That is just a waste of energy. When crafting spells, you must think deeply about what you want. Successful spells require precise goals. Without this in mind, you are aiming energy at a vague objective resulting in partial success. To become a master crafter, you must clarify your goals by sifting through superficial desires and identifying what you want.

Keep your goals achievable and your spells precise. They may not have to rhyme. Not everyone has the knack for verse. Let's break down how beginner, intermediate, and master spell crafters compose a financial aid spell.

Beginner: Bring me more money in a short while.

Intermediate: Bring me a career that offers secure and steady raises at no less than $X annually with regular promotions.

Master: Bring opportunities for secure and steady income streams with a salary of no less than $X monthly after all expenses, bills, investments, and emergencies are covered.

The beginner asked for more money in a short while. This opens the door to literally anything that offers a little more than before. So, they may stumble upon a 20-dollar bill hidden in their back pocket or get a 1-dollar gift card. Not what they hoped for, but not incorrect either, judging by the spell.

With the intermediate caster, there is a stable career. There may be a raise every now and then, but the possibility of expenses eating away at the increased income remains. Every time the salary or a raise comes, boom! Expenses rain down like hailstones, so you have no savings left over.

The master spell lets you tap into all income streams, ensuring money flows steadily rather than a one-time magic trick. The spell was also crafted to remove the possibility of any emergencies waiting to eat away at income accumulated.

Step 2. Think Carefully About the Energies You Wish to Harness as Well as the Desired Outcome Before Composing Your Spell: You want to think of harmonizing the timing in line with astrological influence, lunar phases, and planetary hours to increase the energy of your magic.

Ancient Sumerians and Orthodox magicians designed rites and worship around the five elements (water, air, earth, fire, and ether). They believed each element possessed great symbolism. Ether is also called spirit, as it is said to contain the non-material form of deities, spirits, angels, and other celestial bodies.

Step 3. Maximize the Spell's Power by Being in a Calm Frame of Mind: Frazzled states are not efficient in harnessing and releasing energy. To compose a spell, you must shift your consciousness to quieten the noises in and out of your mind.

Step 4. Raise and Release Energy Toward Your Desire: This is the real foundation of spell casting. Spells gain power by the energy you wield and those present in the ingredients chosen for the spell.

Step 5. Manifest Your Goal: This is the crux, the final stage of spell casting.

Spells can be utilized to solve a lot of life's problems. Yet, many books emphasize spells that address everyday human needs, such as safety, wealth, love, and healing. A reason behind unsuccessful abundance and prosperity spells is the fact that they are fueled by feelings of lust, envy, or greed. There is no doubt that casting spells to solve financial problems is understandable. On the other hand, some needs are valid, and some aren't. Not because they don't exist, but because such lack is rooted in feelings and energies greater than you care to admit.

You can perform spells at any time it pleases you as long as you are:

- **In the Right Frame of Mind:** Distractions and worries affect the focus, which in turn weakens the effect of the spell. Suppressing an emotional reaction like guilt, anger, etc., puts you at risk of issuing commands on the spur of the moment, which is not only irresponsible, but also laden with unforeseen and unpredictable consequences.

- **In Excellent Health:** Ill health is a sign of unbalanced energy. Spells are hard work. Thus, it would help if you had the strength to harness magic. Harnessing power means we have to be at the top of our game health-wise. No one performs an activity to the best of their abilities when they are gravely ill. It is hypocritical to think we can create positive changes while feeling under the weather. The only exception to casting spells in ill health is if they are cast to regain your vitality. In this situation, use calmer spells that require a gentler method of harnessing magic.

When formulating spells, know that everything is essential: the candle color, circle on the ground, the pronunciation of names, herbs involved, the day or hour, the direction you face while chanting, and any incense or oils used are of great significance. Do your best to make sure you get it right or use the proper equivalents of these things for each spell.

The Relevance of Correspondence in Spell Crafting

In spell creation, correspondence is crucial. Correspondences in Wicca are symbols, things, or times that align with specific magical vibrations or energies. Correspondence isn't magic; it benefits magic so that spells are boosted following visualization and the power of intent.

The use of correspondence is a practice as old as time itself. It's said that the more of it that is incorporated into spellwork, the greater the chances of it being successful. For instance, if you are performing a spell to increase creativity, an orange candle is best. Along with oils like cedarwood oil and crystals like citrine, herkimer diamond, or pyrite, you would benefit from invoking the deity of creativity like Athena, Hephaestus, or Kvasir. Spells for creativity are best cast during the waxing or full moon phase to increase chances of success.

Formulating your spells allows you to brainstorm and research. This is the only way you understand what every item, sentence, and component represents. Understanding the significance behind every word uttered and every action performed empowers your intent, which is the most crucial magical ingredient for a spell.

The Ethics of Spellcasting

Spellcasters have a bad rap. They are accused of abusing power for their selfish gain. This is not an attribute linked to only witches or Pagans; humans tend to chuck ethics out the window if they want something. Real spellcasters understand that magic has consequences. Ethics stop them from world domination as we know it. Just because they work in secrecy does not mean they don't have a moral code they abide by.

If you've come this far, you probably know that just because you can summon deities doesn't mean you should break into Cartier's or rob a bank. These are less ethical goals that negate the very foundation of spell casting. Just imagine if everyone in the world decided to use his or her superpowers.

In spell crafting, you must have an idea of what is morally right and wrong. These views must be consistent; otherwise, ethics become invalid. If you are against casting love spells one day and are nose deep into a love potion the next, that breeds inconsistency. Hypocrisy creeps in when you go ballistic at someone who performs similar actions that you do.

Provisional ethics are inescapable sometimes because you may be in a position to choose between two options, so choose the lesser wrong. Other times, the benefits of the many outweigh the needs of the few. Eventually, your moral code exists to make you think deeply about any actions you take in the name of magic and take responsibility for them.

Always bear in mind the importance of free will in magic. When composing spells, do not cast any magic that robs another of their independence. A guideline for spell crafting is that spells must work with the natural order of things, not against them. Only then will they be as successful as you want them to be, and the possibility of errors in judgment reduces.

Ethical Outs

Many spell books instruct on adding a postscript of sorts to spells cast to exempt you from any repercussions. The most common is "by the freewill of all to harm none." This phrase positively reinforces your purity of intent and guards against clauses in spells you unintentionally exclude. With this in mind, understand that your intention, desire, and rationale behind a spell count for more than a codicil at its end that absolves you of responsibility.

Occult books and websites can only offer you so much guidance. You have to learn to trust yourself and your spells. The fact that a sentence is written down in so many texts does not make it faultless. If something does not feel right to you during spell work, don't be afraid to make changes. Although, many times, correspondences like time, lunar association, and deities are carefully thought out due to their association with the spell's intent, modifying one part without a full understanding of its motive within the spell could cause it to lose potency.

Embedded within spell crafting is the concept of responsibility, the natural ally to power. You cannot hold the reins of power and pass on responsibilities to another. Every action has underlying consequences, so if you choose to make and use spells, be prepared to take on the fall out (if any) from the said spell. Before drafting, take time to find out as much information as you can about the situation.

Thinking twice before putting the pen to paper makes certain that you do not make halfhearted or snappy spells. Even in time-sensitive circumstances, you must be calm and sensible. Write rough spells, re-read your notes over and over to check if you still feel the same about the situation or if you have new insight. If you decide to harm another in a fit of rage, make sure you have the spine to bear it when another hurts you in return. The cosmic web of energy never disappoints.

Seal your spell. This is an important aspect of rituals that reinforces your intent. Many Wiccan spell books will advise you to use the words "so mote it be," which is a fancy way of saying "may it be so," like the "amen" for Christians or "selah" for Jews. Create your seal by saying something as simple as "it is done." This sends a signal to your conscious and unconscious mind that the spell is complete, and all you have to do is trust the universe to shift the energies in your favor.

Timing isn't unequivocal, but it could be useful in optimizing your spellwork. If you have an immediate need, make a quick spell. It is not written in stone that certain spells must be performed at a particular time or not at all. If your spell is best when the moon is full, and you have an immediate need, why wait for a full moon? Yes, certain times could boost or jazz up spell potency, but if you are in the middle of a dark moon and you need to cast a spell to heal a beloved pet that seems to be breathing its last, by all means, do it. Healing can take place at any day, time, or lunar phase.

There are no spells to make you forever young or invisible. Those are impossible goals. When crafting a spell, the rule of thumb is to make sure it is achievable without the aid of magic. Then, perform magic to make achieving such goals easier.

To be a successful spell crafter, you must learn to keep detailed records. Crafting spells are similar to chemistry or cooking. It would be best if you kept tweaking for excellent results. The only way you can check how far your skill has evolved is through note taking and record-keeping. Notes on what you used, in what proportions, how long it took for the spell to manifest, and so on will help you in times when you may need to replicate it for yourself or the benefit of another.

Records also allow you to see new techniques you have acquired or developed; times when your power is at its peak; things you need to adjust to change the overall outcome of any spell; and how best to rewrite faulty ones.

Your records should include the following:

- The time and date the spell was performed.
- The direction it was performed.
- The weather at the time.
- The complete spell text.
- Required ingredients.
- Your emotions at the time.
- Short and long-term results.
- Any other pertinent information.

If you added something new in the middle of a spell, take note of it. Take notes of astrological information on the day of the spell, if there was something you excluded or if you came up with a way to improve a spell. These notes are invaluable information for future reference as you evolve as a crafter and caster.

Conclusion

If you are here, I am assuming you read this book cover to cover to discover the multifaceted world of occultism and witchcraft. You now know that understanding the supernatural entails self-conviction, an unbiased mind, desire, patience, and the courage to follow through, as well as the maturity to accept responsibility for every action you take in the name of mysticism.

You can confidently make sound arguments when faced with situations where you have to defend your new beliefs concerning supernatural occurrences and the use of magic. Occultists and witches do not torture children, ride brooms, or shapeshift at will. They also do not belong to fairy tales. They are living, breathing humans, and all around you.

Witchcraft resonates with many of us today because it tackles key issues like overcoming religious bias, care of the environment, gender equality, and the dangers of myopic thinking. Witches and Wiccans alike have one primary goal in mind: improving themselves and the world while working for the greater good using magic. This is all done while understanding their actions affect everything and everyone else.

Magic is all around you. As you tread this path, use all the foundational knowledge acquired from this book to harness the power within yourself. The non-physical realms will forever be open to you so you can get experience. As you noticed, this book cuts through all the flowery language prominent in most texts and states precise methods for practicing magic. There is no right or wrong way to be a witch, so take pride in your craft, listen to your witchy senses, take up your besom and soar.

Authenticity should be a watchword for you as you practice your craft. No two witches are alike. It is this uniqueness, this raw authenticity that is at the heart of witchcraft. Books can only take you so far. If you want to take a step, by all means, do. Fear does nothing but paralyze you. What's the worst that could happen? You get a spell wrong? Haven't we all? Magic is trial and error 90% of the time. Only constant practice will give you increased self-confidence in your abilities and increase your connection with the divine.

Never stop learning. Allow the universe to guide you while you forge your path to self-fulfillment. Practice ethics and never forget the Wiccan Rede that advises us never to use our skill to harm another. Wicca is life changing. As your craft evolves, you will grow and learn from others and easily incorporate your new powers in every moment of your existence. Merry meet, merry part, and blessed be!

Here's another book by Mari Silva that you might like

Your Free Gift (only available for a limited time)

Thanks for getting this book! If you want to learn more about various spirituality topics, then join Mari Silva's community and get a free guided meditation MP3 for awakening your third eye. This guided meditation mp3 is designed to open and strengthen ones third eye so you can experience a higher state of consciousness. Simply visit the link below the image to get started.

https://spiritualityspot.com/meditation

References

Goodrick-Clarke, Nicholas (2008). *The Western Esoteric Traditions: A Historical Introduction.* Oxford: Oxford University Press.

Davis, Erik (2015). *TechGnosis: Myth, Magic & Mysticism in the Age of Information.* North Atlantic Press.

Faivre, Antoine (1994). *Access to Western Esotericism.* SUNY Series in Western Esoteric Traditions. Albany, New York: SUNY Press.

Hanegraaff, Wouter (1996). *New Age Religion and Western Culture: Esotericism in the Mirror of Secular Thought.* Numen Book Series: Studies in the History of Religions. LXXII. Leiden: Brill Publishers.

Hanegraaff, Wouter (2006). "Occult/Occultism". In Wouter Hanegraaff (ed.). *Dictionary of Gnosis and Western Esotericism.* Leiden: Brill Publishers.

Partridge, Christopher (2004). "Occulture". *The Re-Enchantment of the West: Alternative Spiritualities, Sacralization, Popular Culture, and Occulture.* 1. London: T&T Clark.

Partridge, Christopher (2014) [2013]. "Occulture is Ordinary". In Asprem, Egil; Granholm, Kennet (eds.). *Contemporary Esotericism.* Abingdon, Oxford: Routledge.

Partridge, Christopher (ed.) (2014). *The Occult World.* London: Routledge.

Pasi, Marco (2007). "Occultism". In Stuckrad, Kocku von (ed.). *The Brill Dictionary of Religion.* Leiden: Brill Publishers.

Peters, John Durham (2012). *Speaking Into the Air: A History of the Idea of Communication.* University of Chicago Press.

Sconce, Jeffrey (2000). *Haunted Media: Electronic Presence from Telegraphy to Television.* Duke University Press. ISBN 9780822325727.

Dummett, Michael (1980). *The Game of Tarot.* Duckworth, London. ISBN 0 7156 1014 7

Forshaw, Peter, "The Occult Middle Ages", in Christopher Partridge (ed.) (2014). *The Occult World.* London: Routledge. [1]

Kontou, Tatiana – Wilburn, Sarah (ed.) (2012). *The Ashgate Research Companion to Nineteenth-Century Spiritualism and the Occult.* Ashgate, Farnham.

Adler, Margot (2005). *Drawing Down the Moon: Witches, Druids, Goddess-worshippers and Other Pagans in America Today* (third ed.). London: Penguin.

Crowley, Vivianne (1989). *Wicca: The Old Religion in the New Age.* London: Aquarian Press.

Doyle White, Ethan (2016). *Wicca: History, Belief, and Community in Modern Pagan Witchcraft.* Brighton: Sussex Academic

Hanegraaff, Wouter J. (1996). *New Age Religion and Western Culture: Esotericism in the Mirror of Secular Thought.* Leiden: Brill.

Harvey, Graham (2007). *Listening People, Speaking Earth: Contemporary Paganism* (2nd ed.). London: Hurst & Company.

Hutton, Ronald (1991). *The Pagan Religions of the Ancient British Isles: Their Nature and Legacy.*

Hutton, Ronald (1999). *The Triumph of the Moon: A History of Modern Pagan Witchcraft.* Oxford and New York: Oxford University Press.

Lamond, Frederic (2004). *Fifty Years of Wicca.* Sutton Mallet, England: Green Magic.

Orion, Loretta (1994). *Never Again the Burning Times: Paganism Revisited.* Long Grove, Illinois: Waveland Press.

Pearson, Joanne (2002). "The History and Development of Wicca and Paganism". In Joanne Pearson (ed.). *Belief Beyond Boundaries: Wicca, Celtic Spirituality and the New Age.* Aldershot: Ashgate.

Pearson, Joanne (2007). *Wicca and the Christian Heritage: Ritual, Sex and Magic.* London and New York: Routledge.

Ruickbie, Leo (2004). *Witchcraft Out of the Shadows.* London: Hale.

Strmiska, Michael F. (2005). "Modern Paganism in World Cultures". *Modern Paganism in World Cultures: Comparative Perspectives.* Santa Barbara, California: ABC-Clio.

Buckland, Raymond (2002) [1971]. *Witchcraft From The Inside: Origins of the Fastest Growing Religious Movement in America* (3rd ed.). St. Paul, MN: Llewellyn Publications.

Buckland, Raymond (1986). *Buckland's Complete Book of Witchcraft*. St. Paul, MN: Llewellyn.

Farrar, Janet; Farrar, Stewart (1981). *A Witches' Bible: The Complete Witches Handbook*. London: Phoenix Publishing.

Farrar, Janet; Farrar, Stewart (1984). *The Witches' Way: Principles, Rituals and Beliefs of Modern Witchcraft*. Phoenix Publishing.

Gallagher, Ann-Marie (2005). *The Wicca Bible: the Definitive Guide to Magic and the Craft*. New York: Sterling Publishing.

Gardner, Gerald B. (2004) [1959]. *The Meaning of Witchcraft*. Boston: Weiser Books.

Valiente, Doreen (1973). *An ABC of Witchcraft Past and Present*. Robert Hale Ltd.

Bado-Fralick, Nikki (2005). *Coming to the Edge of the Circle: A Wiccan Initiation Ritual*. Oxford University Press.

Heselton, Philip (2000). *Wiccan Roots: Gerald Gardner and the Modern Witchcraft Revival*. Capall Bann.

Clifton, Chas S (2006). *Her Hidden Children: The Rise of Wicca and Paganism in America*. AltaMira Press.

Lamond, Frederic (2004). *Fifty Years of Wicca*. Green Magic.

Gardner, Gerald. (2004). *Witchcraft and the Book of Shadows* Edited by A. R. Naylor. Thame, Oxfordshire: I-H-O Books.

9 781638 180272